ORAL SKILLS FOR LAWYERS

ORAL SKILLS FOR LAWYERS
SECOND EDITION

Katherine Blow and Jacqueline Kempton

Second edition published 2023 by
The University of Law,
2 Bunhill Row
London EC1Y 8HQ

First edition published 2021

British Library Cataloguing in Publication Data

A catalogue record for this book is available from the British Library.

ISBN 978 1 915698 65 0

Preface

The Solicitors Qualifying Examination (SQE) is the new assessment for all aspiring solicitors in England and Wales. They will have to pass both stages of the SQE assessment: SQE1 which focuses on Functioning Legal Knowledge (FLK) and SQE2 which tests practical legal skills and knowledge. This is one of two study manuals that have been specifically designed to support the reader to achieve the SQE2 Assessment Specification. Each manual aims to provide the reader with a thorough knowledge and understanding of the practical legal skills assessed in SQE2.

This study manual covers the Solicitors Regulation Authority (SRA)'s syllabus for the SQE2 assessments in Advocacy and Client Interviewing and Completion of Attendance Note/Legal Analysis. It offers practical guidance on each skill accompanied by realistic examples and/or handy templates. While this manual focuses on mastering the SQE2 oral skills and passing the SQE2 assessments, it also offers some more general advice on developing those skills in professional legal practice.

This manual has been compiled from the version of the SRA's SQE2 Assessment Specification current at the time of writing. The manual is not intended to constitute legal advice. The publisher and writers are not responsible or liable for the results of any person acting (or omitting to act) on the basis of information contained within this publication.

For those readers who are students at The University of Law, this study manual is used alongside other learning resources to best prepare students not only for the SQE2 assessments, but also for a future life in professional legal practice.

We hope you find this manual supportive of your preparation for SQE2 and we wish you every success.

The legal principles and rules contained within this manual are stated as at 1 January 2023.

Author acknowledgements
The authors would like to thank their colleagues at The University of Law for their invaluable help in the preparation of this manual.

Extracts from the SRA's SQE2 Assessment Specification are reproduced with kind permission of the SRA (see https://sqe.sra.org.uk/exam-arrangements/assessment-information).

Contents

1 Introduction to the Oral Skills Assessments

SQE2 syllabus

This chapter summarises the guidance which the SRA has issued on the SQE2 oral skills assessments. There is a corresponding chapter on the SQE2 written skills assessments in The University of Law SQE2 manual *Written Skills for Lawyers*.

While this manual focuses on mastering the SQE2 oral skills and passing the SQE2 assessments, it also offers some more general guidance on developing those skills in legal practice.

1.1 Introduction

This manual looks individually at the two SQE2 oral skills, but it begins by considering themes which are common to both of them. This chapter examines the framework which the SRA has set out for the SQE2 oral assessments. **Chapter 2** deals with oral communication and **Chapter 3** with negotiation.

This chapter looks at:

- the two oral skills;
- the other areas which will be tested pervasively;
- the practicalities of the assessments;
- the Assessment Objectives and Criteria;
- how the assessments are marked;
- the threshold standard;
- the Statement of Solicitor Competence; and
- the Functioning Legal Knowledge required for SQE2.

IMPORTANT. The information below is taken from the SRA's SQE2 Assessment Specification and is correct at time of going to press. However, as this may be updated it is vital that you check the SRA website to view the most up-to-date specification (https://sqe.sra.org.uk/exam-arrangements/assessment-information).

1.2 The oral skills

There are two oral skills which will be assessed in SQE2:

- Client Interviewing and Completion of Attendance Note/Legal Analysis; and
- Advocacy.

There are two further aspects of a solicitor's work, negotiation and ethics and professional conduct, which will not be tested individually but will be assessed in the context of the SQE2 assessments, as per the table below.

Oral skill	Negotiation may be assessed?	Ethical and professional conduct issues may arise?
Client Interviewing and Completion of Attendance Note/Legal Analysis	✓	✓
Advocacy		✓

1.2.1 Negotiation

There is no separate assessment called negotiation, but the SRA has made it clear that all deliveries of SQE2 will contain at least one assessment involving negotiation. You can read more about the skill of negotiation in the context of the SQE2 assessments in **Chapter 3**.

1.2.2 Ethics and professional conduct

Questions on ethics and professional conduct will be pervasive throughout SQE2. The SRA guidance makes it clear that ethical and professional conduct issues will not be flagged, and that candidates will need to identify any such issues and exercise judgment to resolve them honestly and with integrity. The chapters on the individual oral skills in this manual discuss the types of issue which might arise.

1.2.3   The practice areas

The table below shows the practice areas in which the SQE2 oral skills will be assessed and the underlying black letter law on which they may draw. The Functioning Legal Knowledge (FLK) required is considered in more detail at the end of this chapter.

The table also identifies the practice areas in which questions involving Taxation may arise in the SQE2 assessments. The full details can be found in Annex 1 of the SRA's SQE2 Assessment Specification.

Assessment	Practice area	Black letter law	Taxation
Advocacy	Dispute Resolution	Contract Law and Tort	
	Criminal Litigation (including advising clients at the police station)	Criminal Liability	
Client Interviewing and Completion of Attendance Note/Legal Analysis	Property Practice	Land Law	✓
	Wills and Intestacy, Probate Administration and Practice	Trusts	✓

1.3   SQE2 oral assessments – the practicalities

The SQE2 oral skills will be assessed over two assessment days. You can find detailed guidance about these on the SRA website, as well as information about the assessment windows.

1.3.1   Venue

The SQE2 oral assessments will take place at an oral assessment centre, either in London, Manchester or Cardiff. More details are available on the SRA website.

1.3.2   The assessment timetable

The SQE2 oral assessments will take place over two consecutive half-days. You will take a total of four oral skills assessments on the days and in the practice areas indicated in the table below. Each assessment will last for a total of one hour.

Day One	Day Two
Advocacy (*Dispute Resolution*)	Advocacy (*Criminal Litigation*)
Interview and Attendance Note/Legal Analysis (*Property Practice*)	Interview and Attendance Note/Legal Analysis (*Wills and Intestacy, Probate Administration and Practice*)

You may complete the assessments in a different order to that listed. You may therefore start with either the Interview and Attendance Note/Legal Analysis or the Advocacy.

1.3.3 The form of the assessments

The SRA website provides a sample question for each of the SQE2 assessments. These include sample answers A and B, which are both at pass level but of different standards, as well as a discussion of the answer. These are a very useful resource which you can use to familiarise yourself with the way the questions may be framed but do note the SRA's warning at the front of each sample question.

There are no permitted materials for the SQE2 oral assessments. The SRA website gives detail of the equipment (such as a calculator) which will be provided.

Advocacy

You will be given a case study on which you will conduct a piece of courtroom advocacy. An email will ask you to conduct the advocacy and will tell you in which court you will be appearing. Where relevant, you will also be given a file of documents. You may be asked questions during the advocacy. You will have 45 minutes to prepare.

You will then have 15 minutes to make your submission to a judge who is present in the room. The judge will be played by a solicitor of England and Wales who will assess you both on skills and application of law.

Client Interviewing and Completion of Attendance Note/Legal Analysis

This comprises the two stages set out below.

The interview

You will be given an email from a partner or a secretary stating who the client is and providing an indication of what the client has come to discuss. The email may, but will not necessarily, be accompanied by documents. The email may also indicate specific legal issues to which you should have particular regard in the interview and the subsequent attendance note/case analysis.

You will have 10 minutes to consider the email and/or documents.

You will then have 25 minutes to conduct the interview with the client. The client may be, but will not necessarily be, somebody in vulnerable circumstances.

An assessor who will play the role of the client will assess you only on skills (not on application of law).

In the interview you should aim to win the client's trust and confidence. You should try to obtain all the relevant information and as full an understanding as possible of the client's concerns. You do not need to provide detailed advice at this stage. You can conduct the interview on the basis that you will be advising the client in detail at a later date. However, you do need to give enough preliminary advice and to address enough of the client's concerns to establish the client's trust and confidence.

Completion of the attendance note/legal analysis

You will then have 25 minutes to write, by hand, an attendance note/legal analysis of the interview you have just completed. All relevant information obtained during the interview should be recorded in the attendance note/legal analysis. You should provide an analysis of any legal issues that arise in the matter and record your initial advice for the client. The attendance note/legal analysis should also identify the next steps to be taken by the solicitor and, where applicable, the client, as well as any ethical issues that arise and how they should be dealt with. This may (but will not necessarily) include options and strategies for negotiation.

If the email from the partner or secretary has asked you to deal with any specific issues or questions, then advice on these issues should also be included.

1.3.4 Dress code

For the SQE2 oral assessments you should wear clothing suitable for a business environment.

1.4 Assessment Objectives and Criteria

Each of the SQE2 assessments has its own Assessment Objective and Assessment Criteria. These are considered in the relevant chapters of this manual and can also be viewed on the SRA website.

1.4.1 The Assessment Objective

The Assessment Objective sets out in one sentence what the candidate can demonstrate in each assessment

SQE2 oral assessment	Assessment Objective
	Candidates can demonstrate that they are able to...
Advocacy	conduct a piece of advocacy before a judge
Interview	conduct an interview with a client
Attendance note/legal analysis	produce an attendance note recording a client interview and initial legal analysis.

1.4.2 The Assessment Criteria

The Assessment Criteria set out the benchmarks against which you will be assessed in each SQE2 assessment. You will see that for Advocacy and Attendance note/legal analysis these are divided between skills and application of the law, which are given equal weighting in the marking. A separate set of skills criteria is provided for the assessment of the Interview itself.

1.4.2.1 The application of law criteria

The 'application of law' criteria are the same for Advocacy and Attendance note/legal analysis (and for the SQE2 written assessments). These require candidates to:

(1) Apply the law correctly to the client's situation.

(2) Apply the law comprehensively to the client's situation, identifying any ethical and professional conduct issues and exercising judgment to resolve them honestly and with integrity.

The SRA has provided a non-exhaustive list of what applying the 'correct and comprehensive application of the law' criteria might look like, as follows:

• identifying relevant legal principles;

• applying legal principles to factual issues, so as to produce a solution which best addresses a client's needs and reflects the client's commercial or personal circumstances, including as part of a negotiation;

• interpreting, evaluating and applying the results of research;

- ensuring that advice is informed by appropriate legal analysis and identifies the consequences of different options;
- drafting documents which are legally effective;
- applying understanding, critical thinking and analysis to solve problems;
- assessing information to identify key issues and risks;
- recognising inconsistencies and gaps in information;
- evaluating the quality and reliability of information;
- using multiple sources of information to make effective judgments; and
- reaching reasoned decisions supported by relevant evidence.

The SRA has also explained the distinction between 'correct' and 'comprehensive' application of the law. As you might expect, this depends on the extent to which the legal issue has been made clear in your instructions:

> The assessment criteria for application of law refer to legally correct and legally comprehensive. How each of these is interpreted will depend on an academic judgment about each assessment informed by the Statement of Solicitor Competence (Annex 3) and the Functioning Legal Knowledge for SQE2 (Annex 1). For instance, in an assessment where the candidate has to identify the legal issues, credit for this might be given under legally comprehensive. Where the legal issues are made explicit in the question, credit under legally comprehensive might be awarded for giving a comprehensive analysis of those issues, not just for identifying them.

1.5 Marking the SQE2 oral assessments

The Assessment Criteria set out above provide the framework against which the SQE2 oral assessments will be marked. In the interview an assessor who will play the role of the client will assess you only on skills (not on application of law). Otherwise the marking will be carried out by a solicitor, who will have been trained and who will assess candidates on both skills and application of law. The assessor will assess candidates' performance against the criteria using a scale from A to F and making *global professional judgments related to the standard of competency of the assessment'*. The grading will be converted into the marks set out in the table below.

A	Superior performance: well above the competency requirements of the assessment	5
B	Clearly satisfactory: clearly meets the competency requirements of the assessment	4
C	Marginal pass: on balance, just meets the competency requirements of the assessment	3
D	Marginal fail: on balance, just fails to meet the competency requirements of the assessment	2
E	Clearly unsatisfactory: clearly does not meet the competency requirements of the assessment	1
F	Poor performance: well below the competency requirements of the assessment	0

The SRA states that in arriving at a final mark for the candidate across all assessments, skills and application of law are weighted equally and that is to make sure that adequate weighting is given to the quality of the advice provided. To pass SQE2 candidates will need to obtain the overall pass mark for SQE2.

You can find out more about information will be given about the results of the SQE2 assessments from the 'Results and resits' page of the SRA website.

1.6 What standard will you be expected to achieve?

The standard against which you will be assessed is the 'threshold standard', which is the standard of competency of the Day One solicitor. But what does this standard mean and how will it be applied in a consistent way?

1.6.1 The threshold standard

The starting point is the Statement of Solicitor Competence (SoSC), which is a set of competencies which apply to all solicitors. To reflect the development of these competencies throughout a solicitor's career different levels of performance (from 1 to 5) apply at different stages. Candidates for SQE2 are expected to achieve level 3, which is the standard to which the competencies should be performed upon qualification as a solicitor (the 'Day One solicitor').

Annex 2 of the SQE2 Assessment Specification, which is copied below, sets out the level of performance which is expected of a level 3 solicitor in six key areas. You can read more about the threshold standard, and how it compares with the other standards, on the SRA website. You will see that, while a clear standard of competence is expected at level 3, there is also an expectation of development and improvement. For example, under the heading, 'Standard of work' you will see that a level 3 solicitor is expected to *achieve an acceptable standard for straightforward tasks, but complex tasks may lack refinement*. By contrast, at level 4, the expectation is *'Full acceptable standard achieved routinely'* and at level 5 is *'Excellence achieved with ease'*.

Threshold standard

Functioning legal knowledge	Standard of work	Autonomy	Complexity	Perception of context	Innovation and originality
Identifies the legal principles relevant to the area of practice and applies them appropriately and effectively to individual cases.	Acceptable standard achieved routinely for straightforward tasks. Complex tasks may lack refinement.	Achieves most tasks and able to progress legal matters using own judgment, recognising when support is needed.	Able to deal with straightforward transactions, including occasional, unfamiliar tasks which present a range of problems and choices.	Understands the significance of individual actions in the context of the objectives of the transaction/ strategy for the case.	Uses experience to check information provided and to form judgments about possible courses of action and ways forward.

1.6.2 Statement of Solicitor Competence

So, what are the competencies? 'Competence' is defined by the SRA as *'the ability to perform the roles and tasks required by one's job to the expected standard'*. In the SoSC the SRA has set out what solicitors should be able to do in these four key areas:

A. Ethics, professionalism and judgment

B. Technical legal practice

C.   Working with other people

D.   Managing themselves and their own work

In turn, each area is broken down into a series of propositions (A1, A2 etc.) for which examples are provided. For instance, under the heading *'A. Ethics, professionalism and judgment'* the SRA sets out the proposition *'A1. Act honestly and with integrity, in accordance with legal and regulatory requirements and the SRA Standards and Regulations.'* It then provides a list of examples, beginning with:

> *'a. Recognising ethical issues and exercising effective judgment in addressing them.'*

You can find the full SoSC at Annex 3 of the SQE2 Assessment Specification and in the appendix to this chapter.

1.6.3   The competencies mapped against the SQE2 Assessment Specification

Clearly, not all the competencies will apply to all the SQE2 skills. The SRA has therefore mapped the relevant competencies against each one. The result can be found at Annex 4 of the SQE2 Assessment Specification, which is set out in the appendix to this chapter. In particular, in relation to Advocacy, you should note the points listed under B5 *'Undertake effective spoken and written advocacy'* and, in relation to Interview and Attendance Note/ Legal Analysis, the points listed under C5 *'Establish and maintain effective and professional relations with clients'.*

For each of the SQE2 assessments you should check which of the competencies the SRA has identified as being relevant, with a view to demonstrating these in the assessment. This manual provides guidance on how this can be achieved.

1.7   Functioning Legal Knowledge for SQE2

As noted above, the Assessment Criteria for each of the SQE2 oral assessments have been divided between skills and application of law. In arriving at a final mark across all assessments, these are weighted equally. The SRA explains that this is to make sure that adequate weighting is given to the quality of the advice provided.

So, what law will you need to know for the SQE2 oral assessments? As with SQE1, the SRA has set out the FLK required. This can be found at Annex 1 of the SQE2 Assessment Specification, which sets out the legal principles which candidates will be expected to know in relation to the black letter law and the five practice areas assessed in SQE2. It is described by the SRA as a 'subset' of the FLK required for SQE1.

You should refer to the SRA website for the full syllabus for each of these areas, and to your SQE1 materials for the substance of them. If you are feeling daunted by the amount of law to cover, bear in mind the guidance from the SRA below, to reassure you that the focus is not on esoteric legal points. Looking at the sample questions which the SRA has published should also reassure you that the legal points which these cover are familiar to you.

The SRA website provides the following guidance on the level of detail required:

> *In demonstrating that they have reached the standard of competency of a Day One Solicitor, candidates will need to demonstrate that they can apply fundamental legal principles in the skills-based situations covered by SQE2 in a way that addresses the client's needs and concerns. They will need sufficient knowledge to make them competent to practise on the basis that they can look up detail later. Candidates will not be expected to know or address detail that a Day One Solicitor would look up, unless they have been provided with that detail as part of the assessment materials.*

It has further clarified that,

> *The questions in SQE2 are designed to test legal skills within the context of the application of fundamental legal rules and principles at the level required of a competent newly qualified Solicitor. They are not designed to test specialist practice which is unlikely to be encountered at the level of a Day One Solicitor.*

> *Questions test central areas that are clearly covered by the FLK.*

Finally, for SQE1 purposes, the SRA provided that,

> *On occasion in legal practice a case name or statutory provision, for example, is the term normally used to describe a legal principle or an area of law, or a rule or procedural step (e.g. Rylands v Fletcher, CPR Part 36, Section 25 notice). In such circumstances, candidates are required to know and be able to use such case names, statutory provisions etc. In all other circumstances candidates are not required to recall specific case names, or cite statutory or regulatory authorities.*

The same provision arguably applies by analogy to SQE2 but remember that you may be provided with legal materials as part of an SQE2 assessment. In that case you would be expected to refer to any case names and statutory authorities which these contain, as appropriate.

APPENDIX TO CHAPTER 1

The Statement of Solicitor Competence

Annex 3 of the SQE2 Assessment Specification

A.   **Ethics, professionalism and judgment**

A1. Act honestly and with integrity, in accordance with legal and regulatory requirements and the SRA Standards and Regulations, including:

a.   Recognising ethical issues and exercising effective judgment in addressing them.

b.   Understanding and applying the ethical concepts which govern their role and behaviour as a lawyer.

c.   Identifying the relevant SRA Principles and rules of professional conduct and following them.

d.   Resisting pressure to condone, ignore or commit unethical behaviour.

e.   Respecting diversity and acting fairly and inclusively.

A2. Maintain the level of competence and legal knowledge needed to practise effectively, taking into account changes in their role and/or practice context and developments in the law, including:

a.   Taking responsibility for personal learning and development.

b.   Reflecting on and learning from practice and learning from other people.

c.   Accurately evaluating their strengths and limitations in relation to the demands of their work.

d.   Maintaining an adequate and up-to-date understanding of relevant law, policy and practice.

e.   Adapting practice to address developments in the delivery of legal services.

A3. Work within the limits of their competence and the supervision which they need, including:

a.   Disclosing when work is beyond their personal capability.

b.   Recognising when they have made mistakes or are experiencing difficulties and taking appropriate action.

c.   Seeking and making effective use of feedback, guidance and support where needed.

d.   Knowing when to seek expert advice.

A4. Draw on a sufficient detailed knowledge and understanding of their field(s) of work and role in order to practise effectively, including:

a.   Identifying relevant legal principles.

b.   Applying legal principles to factual issues, so as to produce a solution which best addresses a client's needs and reflects the client's commercial or personal circumstances.

c.   Spotting issues that are outside their expertise and taking appropriate action, using both an awareness of a broad base of legal knowledge (insofar as relevant to their practice area) and detailed knowledge of their practice area.

A5. Apply understanding, critical thinking and analysis to solve problems, including:

a.   Assessing information to identify key issues and risks.

b.   Recognising inconsistencies and gaps in information.

c.   Evaluating the quality and reliability of information.

d.   Using multiple sources of information to make effective judgments.

e.   Reaching reasoned decisions supported by relevant evidence.

B.   **Technical legal practice**

B1. Obtain relevant facts, including:

a.   Obtaining relevant information through effective use of questioning and active listening.

b.   Finding, analysing and assessing documents to extract relevant information.

c.   Recognising when additional information is needed.

d.   Interpreting and evaluating information obtained.

e.   Recording and presenting information accurately and clearly.

B2. Undertake legal research, including:

a.   Recognising when legal research is required.

b.   Using appropriate methods and resources to undertake the research.

c.   Identifying, finding and assessing the relevance of sources of law.

d.   Interpreting, evaluating and applying the results of the research.

e.   Recording and presenting the findings accurately and clearly.

B3. Develop and advise on relevant options, strategies and solutions, including:

a.   Understanding and assessing a client's commercial and personal circumstances, their needs, objectives, priorities and constraints.

b.   Ensuring that advice is informed by appropriate legal and factual analysis and identifies the consequences of different options.

B4. Draft documents which are legally effective and accurately reflect the client's instructions including:

a.   Being able to draft documents from scratch as well as making appropriate use of precedents.

b.   Addressing all relevant legal and factual issues.

c.   Complying with appropriate formalities.

d.   Using clear, accurate and succinct language.

B5. Undertake effective spoken and written advocacy, including:

a.   Preparing effectively by identifying and mastering relevant facts and legal principles.

b.   Organising facts to support the argument or position.

c.   Presenting a reasoned argument in a clear, logical, succinct and persuasive way.

d.   Making appropriate reference to legal authority.

e.   Complying with formalities.

f.   Dealing with witnesses appropriately.

g.   Responding effectively to questions or opposing arguments.

h.   Identifying strengths and weaknesses from different parties' perspectives.

B6. Negotiate solutions to clients' issues, including:

a.   Identifying all parties' interests, objectives and limits.

b.   Developing and formulating best options for meeting parties' objectives.

c.   Presenting options for compromise persuasively.

d.   Responding to options presented by the other side.

e.   Developing compromises between options or parties.

B7. Plan, manage and progress legal cases and transactions, including:

a. Applying relevant processes and procedures to progress the matter effectively.

b. Assessing, communicating and managing risk.

c. Bringing the transaction or case to a conclusion.

C. Working with other people

C1. Communicate clearly and effectively, orally and in writing, including:

a. Ensuring that communication achieves its intended objective.

b. Responding to and addressing individual characteristics effectively and sensitively.

c. Using the most appropriate method and style of communication for the situation and the recipient(s).

d. Using clear, succinct and accurate language avoiding unnecessary technical terms.

e. Using formalities appropriate to the context and purpose of the communication.

f. Maintaining the confidentiality and security of communications.

g. Imparting any difficult or unwelcome news clearly and sensitively.

C2. Establish and maintain effective and professional relations with clients, including:

a. Treating clients with courtesy and respect.

b. Providing information in a way that clients can understand, taking into account their personal circumstances and any particular vulnerability.

c. Understanding and responding effectively to clients' particular needs, objectives, priorities and constraints.

d. Identifying and taking reasonable steps to meet the particular service needs of all clients including those in vulnerable circumstances.

e. Identifying possible courses of action and their consequences and assisting clients in reaching a decision.

f. Managing clients' expectations regarding options, the range of possible outcomes, risk and timescales.

g. Agreeing the services that are being provided and a clear basis for charging.

h. Explaining the ethical framework within which the solicitor works.

i. Informing clients in a timely way of key facts and issues including risks, progress towards objectives, and costs.

j. Responding appropriately to clients' concerns and complaints.

C3. Establish and maintain effective and professional relations with other people, including:

a. Treating others with courtesy and respect.

b. Delegating tasks when appropriate to do so.

c. Supervising the work of others effectively.

d. Keeping colleagues informed of progress of work, including any risks or problems.

e. Acknowledging and engaging with others' expertise when appropriate.

f. Being supportive of colleagues and offering advice and assistance when required.

g. Being clear about expectations.

h. Identifying, selecting and, where appropriate, managing external experts or consultants.

D. **Managing themselves and their own work**

D1. Initiate, plan, prioritise and manage work activities and projects to make sure that they are completed efficiently, on time and to an appropriate standard, both in relation to their own work and work that they lead or supervise, including:

a. Clarifying instructions so as to agree the scope and objectives of the work.

b. Taking into account the availability of resources in initiating work activities.

c. Meeting timescales, resource requirements and budgets.

d. Monitoring, and keeping other people informed of, progress.

e. Dealing effectively with unforeseen circumstances.

f. Paying appropriate attention to detail.

D2. Keep, use and maintain accurate, complete and clear records, including:

a. Making effective use of information management systems (whether electronic or hard copy), including storing and retrieving information.

b. Complying with confidentiality, security, data protection and file retention and destruction requirements.

D3. Apply good business practice, including:

a. Demonstrating an adequate understanding of the commercial, organisational and financial context in which they work and their role in it.

b. Understanding the contractual basis on which legal services are provided, including where appropriate how to calculate and manage costs and bill clients.

c. Applying the rules of professional conduct to accounting and financial matters.

d. Managing available resources and using them efficiently.

SQE2 skills mapping against the SQE2 Assessment Specification

Annex 4 of the SQE2 Assessment Specification

SoSC	Client interview and attendance note/legal analysis	Advocacy	Case and matter analysis	Legal writing	Legal research	Legal drafting
A. Ethics						
A1	x	x	x	x	x	x
A2	x	x	x	x	x	x
A3	x	x	x	x	x	x
A4	x	x	x	x	x	x
A5	x	x	x	x	x	x
B. Technical legal practice						
B1	x	x	x	x	x	x
B2					x	
B3	x		x	x	x	
B4						x
B5		x				
B6	x		x	x		
B7	x		x	x		
C. Working with other people						
C1	x	x	x	x	x	x
C2	x		x	x		
C3		x		x		
D. Managing themselves and their own work						
D1	x	x	x	x	x	x
D2	x					
D3	x					

2 Oral Communication Skills

SQE2 syllabus

This chapter will help you to meet the SQE2 Assessment Criteria of 'listen[ing]... and questioning effectively' and using 'appropriate language' in oral communication.

This chapter should be read in conjunction with the chapters on Interviewing and Advocacy.

Learning outcomes

By the end of this chapter you should be able to:

* understand why clear oral communication is vital to the work of a solicitor;
* use the elements of vocal communication;
* demonstrate passive and active listening skills;
* explain the difference between open and closed questions; and
* recognise the impact of 'body language' on effective communication.

2.1   Introduction

The term 'oral communication' is used to describe those interactions between individuals which take place by way of the spoken word. The key skills employed are those of speaking and listening, although these will usually be accompanied by non-verbal elements.

During the working day a solicitor will communicate with a wide variety of individuals. The most obvious occasions when oral communication skills are important are when conducting the 'set pieces' of interviewing clients, negotiating or presenting a case to a court. However, solicitors will also need to communicate with other professionals (such as lawyers, accountants, surveyors, estate agents and police officers), with members of the public (such as witnesses) and, of course, with colleagues in their own organisation. Good oral communication skills are highly valued by firms.

This chapter looks at:

- the importance of oral communication;
- oral vs. written;
- developing oral communication skills;
- vocal communication;
- the listener;
- clarity;
- listening;
- questioning; and
- non-verbal communication.

2.2   The importance of oral communication

From a personal, professional and business perspective, a solicitor should be keen to ensure that they establish a good line of communication with a variety of people.

Employing appropriate skills when communicating with clients is an inherent part of a solicitor's role. In its guidance to members of the public, *Information you should expect to receive from your solicitor*, the SRA states 'effective communication from the very beginning is essential to make sure everything goes smoothly and you don't get any nasty surprises later on. You can communicate with your solicitor in person, by telephone, by email, or any combination of these. It is important that you establish from the start what means of communication you will ordinarily use.' Proper communication with clients will promote satisfaction with the solicitor's service. There will be fewer complaints relating to the standard of service, which in turn allows the solicitor more time to concentrate on generating more business for the firm.

Solicitors also need to establish and maintain good working relationships with their colleagues in the office (whether professional or administrative); a solicitor who acts in a professional manner and is polite and clear when giving instructions and who is prepared to listen will promote a better atmosphere in the office. People who have a happy and professional working environment are generally more productive and provide a better service.

Consulting or instructing members of other professions, representatives of official bodies (e.g. court staff) and interviewing members of the public are all a regular part of a solicitor's daily workload. Effective communication should minimise any delay in getting a response and reduce possible confusion in the interpretation of the solicitor's request, instructions or questions thereby improving the service that a client receives. Using appropriate communication skills will also enhance the solicitor's reputation in the community and amongst the professionals with whom they deal. This will promote more referrals of clients to the solicitor's firm.

In the past it would be fair to say that the written word was the solicitor's preferred method of communication. In recent years, however, there has been a shift towards oral communication. In part this is a result of life becoming more 'immediate'; clients and others want things to happen 'now' and so do not want to wait for letters/emails to be written. Technological advances have also made oral communication much easier and more accessible. Solicitors, clients and others are making increasing use of platforms (such as Facetime, Skype and Zoom) which allow audio/video calling and/or recording.

2.3   Oral vs. written

One element of the skill of effective communication lies in selecting the right method for both the situation and the recipient.

In some situations, the use of oral communication is inevitable: for example, when presenting a case at a court hearing or conducting a client interview. In others employing oral communication may be dictated by the circumstances. For example, if the client has poor literary skills, written communication may not be an option. However, in other cases, such as giving advice to the client or conducting negotiations, there will often be a genuine choice.

Oral communication has a number of advantages over written communication:

- it is immediate – information can be imparted, and responses given quickly and efficiently;
- it is easier to convey intention, motivation, goodwill etc.;
- misunderstandings can be corrected immediately;
- the listener can raise questions;
- it can (usually) incorporate non-verbal elements;
- it can demonstrate self-confidence; and
- its more personal nature makes it the preferred method of conveying 'bad news' or sensitive information.

Oral communication also has some disadvantages:

- there is no formal record of what was said (unless there is an audio/video recording);
- there is no time for reflection;
- there is no opportunity for editing – once said, the words cannot be taken back; and
- it can be more time-consuming.

2.4   Developing oral communication skills

It is important to appreciate that oral communication skills are not contained within a set of strict rules which, if applied, will guarantee success. Oral communication skills are highly personal and subjective. It is a matter of an individual developing their own style, which is natural, effective and true to their personality.

Although oral communication skills are largely based on common sense, people's ability to use them varies enormously. Some people are naturally better than others at communicating, but everyone is capable of improvement. Like any other skill (driving a car, playing a musical instrument, playing a sport), performance can be improved by learning specific skills and techniques, and then practising them.

At first, practising new techniques can feel artificial ('It's just not me'), but after a while the technique usually becomes second nature (like changing gear in a car). However, skills training should not be allowed to suppress natural ability, and it is possible to be, say, a competent interviewer or advocate without necessarily having to perform every technique by the book. It is a question of balance; but success comes through practising sound techniques. Brilliant mavericks are rare.

2.5 Vocal communication

The effectiveness of your oral communication is not just dependent on *what* you say, but *how* you say it. The term 'vocal communication' refers to the way in which you use your voice.

2.5.1 Pitch and volume

Pitch refers to the highness or lowness of voice. Everyone has a natural pitch to their voice. However, if someone is nervous the pitch of their voice often becomes higher. Their nervousness is thereby easily conveyed to the listener and can be interpreted as a lack of confidence.

For most people their natural speech pattern incorporates variations in pitch. Variations in vocal pitch are useful because they help to bring what is being said to life.

Volume refers to the loudness of voice. Rather obviously, in order to communicate effectively you must ensure that you can be heard. In most situations a natural speaking voice will suffice. However, in a large courtroom, for example, it may be necessary to increase volume and project clearly.

2.5.2 Pace

Pace of delivery is important. Most people have a natural tendency to speed up their speaking pace when they are nervous. It is important to fight that tendency. You should aim to speak calmly but steadily. Speaking too quickly will result in the listener being unable to follow what you are saying, especially if you are explaining complex issues or presenting a legal argument; speaking too slowly results in the listener losing interest.

2.5.3 Tone

One of the main advantages of the spoken word over the written word is that it is much easier to convey the appropriate tone. Tone allows the speaker to communicate any number of messages: confidence, empathy, contrition, respect, the seriousness of the situation etc. Tone is especially important when you are not face-to-face with the listener and so there is no possibility of such messages being picked up from your body language. It may be necessary to vary the tone when speaking as the subject matter changes.

Using the right tone helps to ensure that the communication achieves its objective. When speaking in a legal context there is a natural anxiety to 'get the law right' and so to focus exclusively on the content. However, this can result in the delivery deteriorating to a flat monotone. In a client interview this is likely to be interpreted by the listener as demonstrating a lack of interest or concern in their case; before a court the argument being presented is likely to lose its persuasiveness.

2.5.4 Verbal mannerisms

Most people pick up verbal mannerisms which become part of their everyday speech. The mannerisms may be so automatic that the speaker is not even aware of them. However, in a formal context such mannerisms should be avoided as they can detract from what is being said and/or distract the listener. Common examples include peppering speech with the repeated use of an unnecessary word such as 'ok', 'good', 'like', 'yes?' or filling pauses with a prolonged 'erm'.

2.6 The listener

In legal practice it is always necessary for a solicitor to communicate in a way that meets the needs of and/or is appropriate to the particular recipient. The language must cater for the recipient's level of knowledge and understanding. A lay person by definition has no knowledge of the law, so jargon and technical terms are generally to be avoided or, if there is genuinely no alternative, they can be used but must be explained. In contrast, when speaking to another lawyer, using technical language is more acceptable.

The contexts in which oral skills are assessed in SQE2 in a sense represent the most extreme ends of the spectrum. In Interviewing you will be dealing with a client who is likely to have little or no legal knowledge and so you will have to display the skill of explaining legal concepts in a way that the client can understand. In Advocacy your 'audience' could not be more legally sophisticated, and this will require you to display the skill of presenting legal arguments effectively and persuasively whilst maintaining the formalities of the courtroom. These skills are explored in context in the remaining chapters of this manual.

2.7 Clarity

Effective oral communication requires clarity of expression.

In the past solicitors were known for their use of archaic words and Latin phrases. Nowadays most solicitors advocate achieving clarity through the use of plain English. This involves employing clear, succinct and straightforward language and avoiding unnecessary technical terms where these are not appropriate to the recipient.

Shorter sentences are usually easier to understand. However, short sentences can sometimes seem abrupt or discourteous to the listener. It is a matter of striking the right balance.

Clarity is also aided through adopting a logical structure. Good structure makes it easier for the listener to follow and understand what is being said. In a sense it is easier to apply a logical structure when you have the opportunity to plan and prepare what you are going to say, for example when making submissions to the court. Most oral communication, however, is both spontaneous and interactive with little opportunity for planning. Nevertheless, you should still take a moment to think about how to best convey the information you have to impart. It may, for example be best to go straight to the main issue; alternatively, it may be clearer to tackle some preliminary issues first.

2.8 Listening

In order to advise a client, or to persuade an opponent or the court, solicitors have to demonstrate that they have both heard and understood what the other has said. An interesting research statistic is that 92 per cent of solicitors think they are good at listening, but only 67 per cent of their clients would agree (*LexisNexis Bellwether Report 2015: The Age of the Client*).

Listening is an underrated skill which requires considerable concentration. Listening as a solicitor is very different from listening in the context of ordinary social discourse, where interchanges are shorter and more fluid and where there is less need to pick up every nuance or recall precisely what was said.

Most authorities on oral communication skills make a distinction between 'passive listening' and 'active listening'.

2.8.1 Passive listening

Passive listening involves using silences and other unobtrusive signals to encourage the speaker to continue. For example, when interviewing a client or questioning a witness, the solicitor might want to induce the speaker to carry on speaking and thereby perhaps volunteer a crucial piece of information.

Silences can be embarrassing in normal social situations, so many people learn during their upbringing to avoid them. Yet silence is one of the most powerful techniques available to a solicitor. It may require a conscious effort to remain silent for longer than normal in the hope that the speaker will fill the void with more information.

Other non-obtrusive signals a solicitor may give to encourage the speaker to continue include:

- eye contact;
- posture;
- nodding;
- acknowledgements ('Uh, huh'); and
- express invitations ('Go on').

2.8.2 Active listening

Active listening, as the phrase suggests, involves more obtrusive techniques which demonstrate to the other person that the solicitor has both heard and understood.

The most common form of active listening is summarising (i.e. giving a short, clear precis of what the speaker has just said). Like silence, the technique is not regularly employed in social conversations and so requires a conscious effort.

Summarising is also used by solicitors to check the effectiveness of communication in the reverse direction (i.e. that the other person has heard and understood the solicitor).

2.9 Questioning

Questioning skills are well-known tools of the solicitor's trade. Questions may be classified according to the breadth of the response they allow (i.e. as open or closed questions).

2.9.1 Open questions

Open questions give maximum freedom to the person being questioned, they encourage expansion and they do not seek to influence the content of the reply:

> 'So, what happened next?'
> 'What were your reactions to that?'
> 'How did you respond to the offer?'
> 'Why did you do that?'
> 'Tell me about your relationship with the managing director.'
> 'Tell me more about ...'

Open questions do not necessarily have to be worded as questions: 'Tell me ...' is a phrase which can be used to invite an open response.

2.9.2 Closed questions

Closed questions invite a narrow answer, from a few words or a sentence to a 'yes'/'no' reply (sometimes called 'yes/no questions'):

'Were you also carrying a knife?'

'Did you accept the offer?'

One particular form of closed question is the leading question. For example, the questioner might deliberately seek to influence the content of the reply by asking a question which encourages a particular answer: 'So you must have been drunk, mustn't you?'

2.10 Non-verbal communication

2.10.1 Appearance

Whilst the saying may be that 'you can never judge a book by its cover', in reality we make judgments about people all the time based on their appearance. We expect solicitors to look 'professional'. A solicitor who fails to meet that expectation may not inspire confidence and risks what they have to say losing credibility. The dress code for the SQE2 oral assessments requires that you wear clothing suitable for a business environment.

2.10.2 Body language

Non-verbal communication, such as facial expressions, eye contact, posture and gestures, is often referred to collectively as 'body language'.

Facial expressions are the most obvious way of conveying thoughts, emotions, intent etc. These messages will be picked up by the observer even before the speaker says a single word. So, for example, to begin by simply smiling and making eye contact makes for a confident start and enables you to begin to establish the all-important connection with the observer from the outset.

Careful observation of the body language of other people can provide clues as to how they are feeling, or how they are responding to advice or to an argument and may therefore be influential in deciding how to proceed. However, tread cautiously, because the clue might not be conclusive: the interpretation of body language is controversial and is subject to cultural variations. Avoiding eye contact may be regarded as an indication of evasiveness and even a lack of truthfulness in some cultures. In others it may be a sign of politeness and sincerity. Be aware of non-verbal communication, but do not allow it to distract you from everything else.

Similarly, awareness of how your own body language affects both yourself and others can help in deciding how to convey your message more effectively. Although it is sometimes said that one cannot (or should not) 'fake' body language, cause and effect are often interrelated. Sitting with your arms tightly folded and your legs crossed, or nervously drumming your fingers or tapping your foot, can affect your own feelings as well as influencing others' perceptions of you. Sitting or standing in a physically relaxed manner can help you feel more relaxed and convey the impression of confidence to an observer.

3 Interviews in Legal Practice

SQE2 syllabus

This chapter will help you to achieve the SQE2 Assessment Objective of demonstrating that you are able to conduct an interview with a client.

Learning outcomes

By the end of this chapter you should be able to:

- appreciate the importance of interviewing skills in practice;
- recognise the range of skills required when conducting an interview;
- understand the steps that need to be taken when preparing for a client interview; and
- outline a structured approach to a client interview.

3.1 Introduction

A significant proportion of a solicitor's working life is spent conducting interviews with clients, witnesses and others. These interviews will be necessitated by a variety of circumstances and be aimed at achieving a number of purposes: building the client's case, challenging evidence, gaining expert insight etc. Of all such interviews, the first interview with a new client is often the most challenging.

The initial interview is usually the first time the solicitor and client meet. As the old saying goes, you never get a second chance to make a first impression. Making a good first impression is crucial if the solicitor wants the client to feel comfortable enough and confident enough to instruct the solicitor to act for them. This meeting will therefore be the basis upon which the solicitor will start to build a rapport with the client.

The information obtained during the interview will influence the direction that the client's case will follow, so good use of listening, questioning and analytical skills will ensure the solicitor establishes as full a picture as possible. It is also the time to establish the terms and conditions of the retainer so that both solicitor and client understand the work that the solicitor will undertake on the client's behalf.

Chapter 2 explored general oral communication skills. This chapter looks at the approach to conducting client interviews in legal practice. **Chapter 4** goes on to look at how the skills and techniques discussed can be employed in the SQE2 assessments.

Whilst this chapter concentrates on a first interview with a client, the skills discussed will be necessary in any interview and the techniques can be adapted to meet any circumstances.

This chapter looks at:

- the client;
- objectives;
- skills and structure;
- the skills;
- planning for an interview; and
- an overview of the structure.

3.2 The client

3.2.1 Client-focus

The focus of every interview must be the client. The interview is obviously occasioned by a need for some kind of legal assistance; however, it is important for the solicitor to remember that first and foremost they are dealing with a person.

The skill of interviewing requires the solicitor to understand the client, not just know how to address the legal issues that they face. A matter which from a legal perspective may be straightforward or routine will be of immense significance for the client. For example, a domestic conveyancing matter may be routine for the solicitor, but the client is likely to be undertaking the largest financial transaction of their life and view the subject matter, not just as a place to live, but as their refuge or sanctuary.

Clients may be going through the same legal process, but each will react differently: one client may view buying a property as an exciting step in life; another may find it devastating if the purchase has been triggered by a relationship breakdown or a death in the family. It is only by gaining a thorough understanding of the individual client and their circumstances that the solicitor will be able to ensure that the legal services they provide are truly targeted at meeting that client's needs and objectives.

3.2.2 Vulnerability

In its guidance *Meeting the Needs of Vulnerable Clients* (29 November 2022) the Law Society says, 'Solicitors need to adapt their practices to identify and meet the needs of clients who may be vulnerable, due to their personal circumstances and barriers put in place by society'. Similarly, the SRA highlights the provision of legal services to those who are vulnerable in its Statement of Solicitor Competence (C2): 'identifying and taking reasonable steps to meet the particular service needs of all clients including those in vulnerable circumstances' (see **Chapter 1**).

The term 'vulnerable' is a broad one. According to the Law Society it extends to anyone who is at a disadvantage because of factors which affect their access to, and use of, legal services. The SRA *Enforcement Strategy* states:

> Vulnerability is not static: it may be short term, or permanent; and may result from the structure of the market, the nature of legal services, the client's personal circumstances, or a combination of factors. Corporate clients may have large in-house teams and be sophisticated purchasers of legal services – but may also be vulnerable in some transactions or circumstances.

In some instances, the link between the client's circumstances and their ability to use legal services is obvious, for example where the client is a child or has a mental impairment. Others less so, for example a client may have difficulty in using legal services as a result of a low income, limited literacy skills or a recent bereavement.

In practice it is a matter of being alert to circumstances which are likely to place the client in a vulnerable situation and responding accordingly. For example, if the client has limited literacy skills the solicitor will need to adjust their methods of communication to meet that client's needs; similarly, if the client has learning difficulties the solicitor will need to take particular care in the wording they use to frame their advice. A client who is in vulnerable circumstances has the same right to expect a proper level of legal services as any other and it is incumbent upon the solicitor to make sure that they receive it.

3.3 Objectives

In legal practice there are usually five main objectives when conducting a first interview with a client (other types of interview may have more limited objectives):

- to establish a good relationship (or rapport) between solicitor and client;
- to obtain relevant information from the client;
- to help the client make appropriate decisions;
- to plan future action; and
- to deal with client care and costs information issues.

3.4 Skills and structure

3.4.1 Interviewing skills

Achieving the objectives referred to at **3.3** requires the effective use of a wide range of skills. The principal skills involved in interviewing a client are:

- listening;
- questioning;
- analysing;

- explaining; and
- note-taking.

3.4.2 Structure outline

The objectives at **3.3** are easier to achieve if the interview is conducted in a logical and coherent manner. There is no set method for conducting a client interview. Indeed, it would be fair to say that most solicitors develop their own personal style over time. However, it is advisable, particularly when the solicitor is not familiar with conducting interviews, to follow an appropriate model.

A 'model' is merely a predetermined structure, which divides the interview into a logical sequence of stages. Each stage involves the performance of certain tasks and requires the use of different combinations of the skills referred to above.

The suggested model used in this manual is:

(1)	GREETING
(2)	OPENING
(3)	LISTENING/OBTAINING THE RELEVANT INFORMATION
(4)	FILLING IN THE DETAIL
(5)	ADVISING
(6)	CLOSING

The model is easy to follow and can be used in any legal context, although the length of time spent on each stage will vary depending on the nature of the client's matter.

The model is considered in more detail at **3.7**.

3.5 The skills

3.5.1 Listening

Listening is an undervalued skill, but it is a key aspect of any client interview.

It is an obvious point, but it is through listening that the solicitor obtains the information they need from the client. Allowing a client to talk and listening carefully to what they have to say is generally a more effective way of gathering information than subjecting them to a rapid succession of questions and noting down the answers. The skill of listening requires a range of techniques to be employed with the aim of sustaining information giving. If a client is verbose, the solicitor may need to adopt a more forceful braking role, but this should occur only when absolutely necessary.

Listening is also vital in gaining the client's trust and confidence. It is essential that throughout the interview the client feels that they are being heard and understood. Employing effective listening techniques will enable the solicitor to demonstrate that this is indeed the case.

3.5.1.1 Acknowledgements

These are brief indications (without interrupting) showing attention, interest and understanding, such as:

'Yes, I see'

'... in France?'

'Mhmmmm'

3.5.1.2   Invitations to continue/elaborate

Examples are:

'Go on'

'What happened?'

'Tell me more about that'

3.5.1.3   Reflecting feeling

This involves the solicitor making it clear that they understand how the client feels, for example, 'I can quite see why you feel so angry about this' or 'I can hear that this is really important to you'. It involves expressing empathy with the client's feelings; not being judgmental about them.

The technique is particularly important where a client's emotions could be a major factor in the case, for example where the client has recently been bereaved. However, reflecting feeling may also be appropriate in interviews which may appear to be less personal, for example when a client has anxieties about the repercussions of a transaction falling through.

3.5.1.4   Silence

In everyday conversation, periods of silence can sometimes seem awkward and even cause embarrassment. However, in an interview, these periods give a client time to recall facts and to organise their thoughts so that they are better able to tell the story as they remember it and to express the feelings it creates. It is therefore important for the solicitor to control the natural urge to fill silences.

3.5.1.5   Body language

A solicitor can gain valuable insights into a client's feelings by observing and correctly interpreting their body language, not merely from listening to their words and tone of voice.

It is also important for the solicitor to think about how their own body language may encourage/discourage information giving and help/hinder good rapport. For example:

- friendly eye contact is positive, but a prolonged stare will be unsettling;
- leaning slightly towards the client shows attentiveness, but care must be taken not to become intimidating;
- head-nodding shows understanding, but will be off-putting if done to excess;
- it goes without saying that irritating/distracting mannerisms must be avoided, for example, pen-tapping, foot-drumming, reading while the client is speaking, etc.

3.5.2   Questioning

In an initial interview, the solicitor needs to obtain information on:

- the nature of the client's problem or proposed transaction;
- the relevant background facts; and
- the client's feelings and objectives.

Whilst much of this may be obtained through use of the listening techniques discussed above, it will invariably be necessary to elicit further information by questioning.

An important preliminary point is to avoid asking more than one question at a time and to ensure that all questions are expressed clearly and succinctly. Questions which are vague, ambiguous or overly complex may confuse a client, but they also suggest a lack of clarity of thought on the part of the solicitor and so risk damaging rapport.

3.5.2.1 Open vs. closed questions

Open questions

The advantages of open questions are that they:

- allow a client to select the subject matter;
- allow a client to select the information they believe to be relevant;
- allow a client to start with information about which they feel comfortable;
- enable a client to articulate their feelings;
- give a client freedom to reflect and to feel more actively involved in the interview; and
- encourage memory by association, which may produce information which would be overlooked if a client were asked only closed questions.

The use of open questions usually enables a great deal of information to be gathered relatively quickly and so allow the solicitor to form an overview of the client's situation and the nature of their instructions. However, open questions also have disadvantages:

- they may initially produce insufficient information;
- they may encourage a client to verbosity and/or irrelevance;
- they may inhibit a reticent client.

Closed questions

The advantages of closed questions are that they:

- are a good method of obtaining precise details;
- may guide a client less stressfully through a sensitive area;
- may give confidence to an initially reticent or anxious client;
- may help to prompt memory;
- help to clarify and probe areas of ambiguity or uncertainty; and
- may quieten a verbose client.

The use of closed questions enables the solicitor to elicit the detail of the client's instructions. However closed questions also have disadvantages:

- they may lead to an over-clinical or 'processing' style of interview;
- they may deprive a client of the opportunity to state the case in their own words;
- they may inhibit rapport;
- they reduce the opportunity to listen to and observe a client, and to understand their needs;
- important areas of information may be missed because a client is not allowed to associate ideas freely; and
- they may result in the interview being directed down a totally irrelevant path.

3.5.2.2 The 'T-funnel'

It will be evident from the above that the use of open questions alone or closed questions alone will not elicit the range of information required or successfully identify the client's needs. However, by combining the two techniques, the solicitor will be able to achieve a thorough exploration of the client's situation.

In the early stages of an interview open questions are normally more advantageous than closed questions. Asking closed questions too early or too often is usually an inefficient way of gathering information and risks the interview feeling more like an interrogation from a client's point of view. Closed questions are usually best employed later in the interview to address points of detail omitted by a client.

The use of open questions followed by closed questions is sometimes known as the T-funnel sequence of questioning:

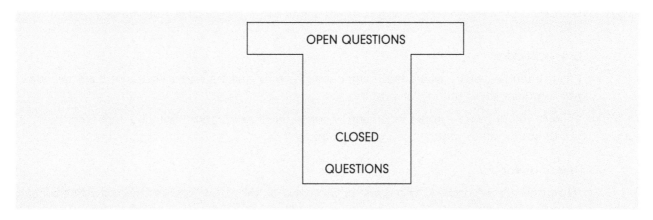

Following the T-funnel approach involves introducing a particular topic with a series of open questions. Only after the open questions cease to be productive should they be narrowed into closed questions.

3.5.2.3   Further clarification and probing

The effective use of a combination of open and closed questions may elicit all the information required. However, it may be necessary to probe even further:

- to resolve areas of ambiguity;
- to jog a client's memory;
- to clarify a client's needs and reaction to the consequences of a proposed course of action; and
- to discover how a client will respond to any legal processes involved (such as litigation) or to possible developments in a transaction (such as a counter-offer in a negotiation).

The following are some techniques which can be employed to achieve these objectives.

Going back one stage

This involves taking a client back one stage in the narrative and inviting them to relive the sequence of events in order to jog the memory:

> Take me through that again but starting from the point when your sister handed the will to your mother for signing.

> Explain what you did about the disrepair beginning from when you first became aware of it.

This technique is useful, as it encourages the client to fill in any gaps in the narrative.

Leading questions

Leading questions can be a useful way of helping clients to convey something which they may have difficulty articulating in their own words:

'So, you've had a difficult relationship with your mother for some time?'

'So, you didn't think it important to tell the landlord?'

'So, you didn't read it before you signed it?'

Prefacing a question with an explanation

This can counteract a client perceiving that a question is irrelevant or allay a client's anxiety in a sensitive area. For example:

> It may be that the tenant will pay up, but if not, we might have to take some other action against them. For that reason, I need to ask you some questions about the tenant's business and financial situation.

There is, however, a danger that the explanation may influence (and therefore distort) the client's reply.

Cross-checking

This is often necessary where the information given by a client reveals gaps or contradictions which require explanation. For example:

> Are you quite sure about that date, because that would mean that the property was flooded before contracts were exchanged?

Devil's advocate

To play devil's advocate is to suggest to a client a different and adverse interpretation of their story. For example:

> You say that you were very close to your father. If that's the case, why hadn't you visited him in the care home?

It is generally advisable for the solicitor to explain why they are doing this because, otherwise, the solicitor's apparent hostility is likely to damage rapport. For example:

> I'm sorry to ask you so bluntly but it's an issue that your step-mother's solicitor is bound to raise in the negotiations.

Summarising

This is an extremely important and useful technique. Its purpose is to double-check that the solicitor's understanding of the facts and of the client's feelings and concerns is correct.

It is useful to summarise the key facts before moving on to the stage of advising the client. For example:

> Now before we talk about what needs to be done let me just check with you that I have got a correct and complete list of your father's assets.

Apart from giving the client an opportunity to correct errors and supply additional facts, summarising reassures them that the solicitor has heard and understood what they have been told. It also gives the solicitor a useful breathing space to think about the matter and the advice that needs to be given. It may also identify some areas on which further questioning is needed before the solicitor can safely advise.

Summarising the solicitor's understanding of the client's feelings and objectives is just as important as summarising factual information:

> So, let me see whether I've correctly understood what you are hoping to achieve out of all this ...

> So, would it be fair to say that maintaining a good relationship with your sister is your main priority?

3.5.3 Analysing

As the facts and client's goals are being identified, the solicitor must analyse which facts and legal principles are relevant, how the law applies to those facts and so reach a conclusion about the client's position and, if necessary, the range of available courses of action.

The process of identifying the issues and the relevant legal principles, then applying the law to the facts in order to reach a conclusion is a normal feature of the academic stage of legal studies. For example, traditional examinations often involve problem-solving questions. The approach is the same in a client interview. An obvious difference, however, is that in a client interview the solicitor has to elicit the relevant information rather than having it presented in the form of a given scenario. There is also little or no time for quiet reflection before being expected to offer at least a tentative view of the position.

The effective use of the listening and questioning techniques described above will enable the solicitor to obtain the required information from the client. As each piece of information is revealed, the solicitor should be analysing it and starting to frame advice. At quite an early stage, the solicitor will probably be able to form a provisional theory about the likely end position. These initial thoughts will help the solicitor identify further questions they need to ask, and these ideas will inevitably have to be reviewed and modified as additional information emerges. The solicitor must be careful to avoid reaching a conclusion until they have a complete picture of the client's situation.

3.5.4 Explaining

Once the solicitor has analysed the client's position, a number of matters will usually have to be explained before a client can be expected to make any decisions required and give instructions.

The solicitor will need to explain the client's legal position. Explaining the relevant law frequently involves explaining concepts which are second nature to the solicitor and which they would normally express in legal terminology (such as 'consideration', 'easements', etc.). It is therefore easy to overlook the simple fact that concepts and terminology which seem quite straightforward to the solicitor can be totally bewildering and meaningless to a lay client. Clarity is vital, and legal jargon should therefore be avoided.

The solicitor may also need to explain the legal procedures which must be followed. The client must understand the steps that need to be followed in order to achieve their desired outcome. Again, these procedures may be familiar to the solicitor, but will be confusing to a client. The solicitor should choose simple, straightforward and jargon-free language.

The ability to present legal concepts in an accessible way is key to building client confidence. Couching advice in clear, simple English with short sentences facilitates understanding. A client who understands the advice given will be in a position to discuss the implications with the solicitor and feel fully involved in the process.

It is often helpful for the solicitor to ask a client whether what they have said has been understood and to offer to repeat the advice. If overdone, this technique may appear patronising. However, if used appropriately, even the most self-confident client will appreciate the solicitor's concern, and a more timid client, who may be reluctant to ask directly, will welcome a genuine offer of clarification.

The solicitor should also bear in mind that, even when they have explained matters clearly, it is often unrealistic to expect a client to remember everything once the interview is over. For this reason, it is desirable in most cases in legal practice to send a follow-up letter to a client summarising the advice given.

3.5.5 Note-taking

Note-taking is an important and difficult skill. No solicitor can memorise every piece of information on all their files, and there may be occasions when another member of the firm will need to take over the file permanently or temporarily. The file must therefore contain a complete, accurate and legible record of the interview. This is best achieved by taking manuscript notes during the interview itself and having a fuller and/or clearer version written up afterwards (see **Chapter 5**).

During a client interview the solicitor will need to take a contemporaneous note which is sufficiently detailed to enable them to make a full attendance note later on. The contemporaneous notes must, at minimum, be sufficient to operate as an aide memoire of the vital facts, names, dates, assets, etc. from which a fuller record can be prepared.

Making a contemporaneous note is important. However, difficulties can arise if detailed notes are made too early in the interview. Writing while a client is explaining the reason for their visit can damage rapport for two reasons. First, it is very difficult for the solicitor to follow the meaning of what the client is saying if they are frantically trying to translate it into a written note. Secondly, it is impossible to write at length without losing eye contact with a client. Few things are more off-putting for a client than trying to relate a story to the top of someone's head. On the other hand, it can be equally off-putting if the solicitor interrupts the flow of a client's narrative by requesting time to write everything down.

To avoid such problems, it is usually advisable to avoid taking notes whilst a client is giving their account of their situation; instead, it is usually preferrable to concentrate on listening to the client's version of events and defer taking notes until later on. However, there is no absolute bar on taking notes early on in the interview. The solicitor simply needs to ensure that doing so does not detract from rapport, perhaps by restricting note-taking to brief jottings which do not destroy eye contact but which will serve at a later stage as a reminder of topics which need to be expanded.

Even when fuller note-taking starts, the solicitor should try to adopt a concise style and be selective about what they write down. Headings can be used effectively to give a structure to the notes. The solicitor should ensure that key names, addresses, figures, dates and verbatim accounts of conversations are accurately worded.

3.6 Planning for an initial interview

3.6.1 The environment

It is important that a client interview takes place in an environment which will help rather than hinder effective communication. The aim should be to create an atmosphere in which the client will feel calm and relaxed, and which will give a favourable impression of both the solicitor and the firm.

In legal practice it will be necessary to ensure that:

- the client will feel comfortable (physically and emotionally);
- the interview will be free from unnecessary interruptions; and
- the office surroundings convey a sense of well-organised professionalism without being austere and/or impersonal.

As a matter of professional conduct solicitors are required to conduct business in a manner that 'encourages equality, diversity and inclusion' (Principle 6). The environment in which the interview takes place should take into account any specific needs of the client, for example the need for wheelchair access or difficulties arising from being hard of hearing.

Seating arrangements may help or hinder effective communication. Views on this topic differ, and an arrangement which seems friendly and welcoming to one client may strike another as over-familiar or even invasive.

However, as far as possible, the arrangement should be one in which:

- the solicitor and client can see and hear each other clearly (this is especially important in the case of clients who are deaf/hard of hearing and may be reliant on lip reading or sign language);
- a client does not feel kept at a distance at one extreme or invaded at the other; and

- the solicitor and (if necessary) the client can make written notes in comfort.

The above comments presuppose that the interview will take place in an environment over which the solicitor has some degree of control, but the interview may, for a variety of reasons, take place in surroundings over which the solicitor will have little or no control. Nevertheless, the client's needs must still be accommodated. It should be possible, for example, to ensure the solicitor seats themself so that they and the client can see and hear each other.

3.6.2 Conflict and identity checks

In its Practice Note *Client Information Requirements* (8 September 2021) The Law Society recommends that, before the initial interview, 'you should obtain information to enable you to carry out necessary background and regulatory checks'.

Paragraph 6 SRA Code of Conduct for Solicitors, RELs and RFLs provides that, generally, a solicitor must not act for a client if there is a conflict of interest, or a significant risk of a conflict of interest, with a current client. A firm should have processes in place to ensure that basic information is obtained from a client when the appointment is made. This information will enable the firm to carry out a conflict check to ensure that there will be no risk of a conflict of interest arising if the firm accepts instructions from this client. If the client does not book an appointment in advance, then this information should still be obtained, and a conflict check carried out before the interview proceeds.

Paragraph 8.1 SRA Code of Conduct for Solicitors, RELs and RFLs requires that 'you identify who you are acting for in relation to any matter'. At one level this means that a solicitor must be clear on whether, for example, they are being instructed by a company as a legal entity or by one of its directors in a personal capacity. However, the primary purpose of Paragraph 8.1 is to prevent fraud. The requirement to establish that a client is in fact who they claim to be is intended to ensure that the solicitor does not fall victim to fraudsters.

In addition, where the Money Laundering, Terrorist Financing and Transfer of Funds (Information on the Payer) Regulations 2017 apply (as will usually be the case for most solicitors) the firm must carry out appropriate due diligence. A new client should be warned when booking the appointment that the firm will need evidence of their identity. A client should be asked to bring proof of identity to the interview. Generally speaking, a solicitor must not accept instructions from a new client involved in regulated activities until due diligence has been carried out.

For detailed information see The University of Law SQE1 manuals *Legal Services* and *Ethics and Professional Conduct*.

3.6.3 Research

In legal practice if a client has instructed the firm before, it will facilitate good rapport and promote the efficient use of both the solicitor's and the client's time if, as far as possible, the solicitor familiarises themself with the client's circumstances. The solicitor should research the client's case history and talk to colleagues who have dealt with the client before. In the case of a new client, it may still be possible to obtain some background information on the client (and, where relevant, the client's business).

A client may provide documents in advance of the interview. Indeed, in some cases it may be useful to request such documents. The document provided by a client may provide an indication of the law that is likely to be relevant to the case and, if appropriate, enable some legal research on that area of law in advance of the interview. However, in anticipating what may be relevant, care must be taken not to pre-judge the issues.

Some firms use case management systems which enable the client to submit a good deal of information to the firm online in advance of the interview. This information must obviously be studied carefully. It will damage rapport to ask for information at the meeting which the client has taken the time and trouble to provide already.

3.6.4 Checklists

Some interviews lend themselves to the use of checklists. If the solicitor knows in advance why a client is coming to see them, it is possible to anticipate the topics that may be relevant to their case. Therefore, through careful planning the solicitor could draw up a checklist to use during an interview as an aide memoire.

Used appropriately, a checklist has the obvious advantage that essential information is unlikely to be overlooked. A checklist also provides the solicitor with a concise and convenient source of information for speedy future reference. However, interviewing a client simply by running through a checklist, particularly at the beginning of the interview, may inhibit effective communication. It may give the appearance of merely 'processing a case' rather than listening to the client's unique personal problem.

Using a checklist in such a manner may damage rapport. A client may get the feeling that they are not being listened to if the questions jump from one topic to another rather than follow up on their current train of thought. Indeed, premature use of a checklist (i.e. before a correct diagnosis of the case has been made) can waste valuable time while a mass of irrelevant information is accumulated.

3.6.5 Interpreters

It is important to establish whether a client has any specific needs relating to their ability to communicate. It may be necessary to use a language or sign language interpreter, for example if a client does not speak the same language as the solicitor or if they have a hearing impairment. Ideally this should be established in advance so that appropriate arrangements are already in place by the time of the interview.

3.6.6 Client care information sheet

The SRA Code of Conduct for Solicitors, RELs and RFLs requires certain information to be given to a client 'at the time of engagement'. For example: how the firm is regulated and the regulatory protections available (Paragraphs 8.10 and 8.11); the client's right to complain and how to complain (Paragraphs 8.3 and 8.4); the likely overall costs of the matter (Paragraph 8.7). For detailed information see The University of Law SQE1 manual *Ethics and Professional Conduct*.

It is usually sensible and convenient for such information to be incorporated into a pre-prepared information sheet, standard client care letter or equivalent. The information sheet can then be explained to a client during the initial interview; they should be asked to sign and date it. A copy of the signed document should be kept by the firm.

3.6.7 No interruptions

It goes without saying that any form of interruption during an interview will immediately convey the impression that a client is not the solicitor's focus and priority. Even the background sound of an incoming email or text will be an irritating distraction. So, colleagues should be made aware that the interview is taking place and computers, laptops and phones turned off or put on silent.

3.7 An overview of the structure

Having a clear idea of how to structure and manage the interview is the key to retaining control and ensuring that all necessary matters are properly addressed. The following checklist provides a handy overview of the stages of the suggested model for a first client interview.

Not every point in the checklist will have to be covered in every client interview. A client interview is unique to that particular client and ultimately must be driven by that client's individual needs. However, keeping the overall structure in mind, understanding what each stage is intended to achieve and why, will enable the solicitor to progress an interview in a logical, coherent and effective manner.

A more detailed explanation of each stage of the model and how they may be applied in the SQE2 assessments is given in **Chapter 4**.

1. Greeting

    Meet, greet and seat the client appropriately and begin to establish good rapport

2. Opening

    (a) Check the reason for the client's visit by way of a closed question

    (b) Outline the proposed structure of interview

    (c) Explain the cost of the interview and any other client care matters

3. Listening/Obtaining the relevant information

    Let the client explain the reason for their visit; use open questions and listening techniques (and avoid note-taking)

4. Fill in detail

    (a) Clarify and fill gaps in the facts using the T-funnel approach

    (b) Identify and explore the client's concerns

    (c) Summarise (a) and (b)

5. Advising

    (a) Outline relevant law and procedure clearly, accurately and comprehensively, taking into account all relevant factual, practical and legal issues

    (b) Address any specific questions or concerns raised by the client

    (c) Discuss the main options (legal and non-legal) to resolve issues or achieve client's objectives including advantages or disadvantages/outline procedural or transactional steps/help client to reach a decision or give instructions/agree a plan of action

6. Closing

    (a) Confirm the follow-up tasks of both solicitor and client

    (b) Give the name of an alternative contact within firm

    (c) Estimate the time frame for the matter

    (d) Give the best information possible relating to the costs of the matter

    (e) Discuss next contact including whether a further meeting is necessary and, if one is needed, when is it likely to be and who is responsible for arranging it

    (f) Parting

4 Conducting a Client Interview

SQE2 syllabus

This chapter will help you to achieve the SQE2 Assessment Objective of demonstrating that you are able to conduct an interview with a client.

Learning outcomes

By the end of this chapter you will be able to:

- plan a structured approach to a client interview;
- recognise the purpose of each stage of a structured interview;
- identify the skills which are appropriate for each stage of a structured interview; and
- use appropriate listening and questioning techniques.

4.1 Introduction

The SQE2 Client Interviewing and Completion of Attendance Note/Legal Analysis assessments comprise two parts:

- conducting a client interview; and

- making a full attendance note.

Chapter 2 considered general oral communication skills and **Chapter 3** explored client interviews in legal practice. This chapter looks at the process of conducting a client interview and considers the specific requirements of the SQE2 Assessment Criteria. Attendance notes will be considered in **Chapter 5**.

The coverage in this chapter is deliberately comprehensive. All stages of the suggested model for a client interview (see **3.7**) are considered fully. In practice the nature of a client's case may result in a particular stage assuming greater or lesser importance or, indeed, becoming redundant. The same is true of the SQE2 assessments. Added to which, elements which would normally feature in a 'real' client interview may be expressly removed or curtailed for assessment purposes.

This chapter looks at:

- the assessment;

- preparation;

- the 'client';

- the interview;

- trust and confidence;

- ethics and professional conduct issues;

- negotiation;

- contemporaneous notes; and

- time management.

4.2 The SQE2 assessments

4.2.1 Form

In the SQE2 assessments candidates will be required to prepare for and then conduct an interview with a client. This part of the assessment therefore takes the form of a role-play, with the candidate acting as the solicitor and a trained assessor taking the role of the client.

Candidates will sit a total of two Interviewing assessments in the practice areas below. Questions in these practice areas may draw on underlying black letter law in the Functioning Legal Knowledge shown in brackets next to each one:

- one in the context of Property Practice *(Land Law)*; and

- one in the context of Wills and Intestacy, Probate Administration and Practice *(Trusts)*.

The assessments may involve negotiation (see The University of Law manual *Written Skills for Lawyers*, Chapter 3). Remember that questions on ethics and professional conduct will be pervasive throughout SQE2.

(See the SRA website for the full syllabus.)

Candidates will receive their instructions for each assessment in the form of an email from a partner or a secretary which will give the client's name and an indication of the reason for the interview. The email may be accompanied by a document or documents.

Candidates will have 10 minutes to prepare and then 25 minutes to conduct the interview (immediately followed by a further 25 minutes to write up the attendance note (see **Chapter 5**)).

4.2.2 Criteria

In the SQE2 assessments candidates will be assessed against the following Assessment Criteria:

Skills

(1) Listen to the client and use questioning effectively to enable the client to tell the solicitor what is important to them.

(2) Communicate and explain in a way that is suitable for the client to understand.

(3) Conduct themselves in a professional manner and treat the client with courtesy, respect and politeness including respecting diversity where relevant.

(4) Demonstrate client-focus in their approach to the client and the issues (i.e. demonstrate an understanding of the problem from the client's point of view and what the client wants to achieve, not just from a legal perspective).

(5) Establish and maintain an effective relationship with the client so as to build trust and confidence.

Note that during this part of the assessment candidates are being assessed on their interviewing skills rather than the law.

You can read more about the SQE2 assessments in **Chapter 1**. In the appendix to that chapter you can see how the Statement of Solicitor Competence applies to the skill of Interviewing.

4.3 Preparation

4.3.1 In advance of the assessment

It is an obvious point, but a key aspect of preparing for the SQE2 assessments is to ensure that you are confident in your knowledge of the law. Although during the first part of assessment you will only be assessed on your interviewing skills, if you are weak on the law this is likely to affect your performance: questions may lack focus, advice may be tentative or incomplete etc. Remember, however, that the level of knowledge required for the assessment is that of a 'Day One' solicitor. If the interview requires knowledge of an aspect of the law which a Day One solicitor would have to look up, this will be provided to you in the assessment.

By the same token, it is important not to become preoccupied with the law to the exclusion of all else. 'Getting the law right' will not in itself guarantee success in the assessment. As part of your preparation, you should do all you can to develop your interviewing skills. Part of that process is understanding what skills are required of you, but practising those skills is also vital. You should take advantage of every opportunity you have to practise elements of the interview or create such opportunities for yourself (for example, ask a friend or colleague to play the role of the client, perhaps using the SRA sample assessment as a scenario); practice elements of the interview, for example explaining legal concepts to a lay person; critically review a recording of yourself 'talking to camera'. The key point is that you should not leave it until the SQE2 assessment itself to try out your interviewing skills for the first time.

As with all the SQE2 assessments, the potential subject-coverage is such that you will not be able to predict the precise content of the assessment with any certainty. You are likely to feel this more acutely in the Interviewing assessment where you are expected to 'perform'. You can, however, think about possible scenarios (such as the client who is buying a house, or the client who needs advice on the distribution of an estate), the information that will be relevant and the type of questions you will need to ask. Although remember that mechanically following a checklist, even a mental one, can impede the interview (see **3.6.4**).

4.3.2 In the assessment

At the start of the SQE2 assessment you will be handed instructions in the form of an email from a secretary or partner and given 10 minutes to prepare to conduct the interview. Your preparation time is therefore short, and you should plan in advance how you will be able to use it effectively.

As a first point look at the instructions for any information given about the assessment itself. Your instructions may state, for example, that you do not need to deal with costs and client care. If that is the case, then you can mentally put those issues to one side and ignore the steps in the interviewing model which deal with them.

The instructions will give you the client's name. Commit this to memory as you will need to use it to greet the client at the beginning of the interview.

The instructions will also provide at least some indication of the reason for the meeting. This will enable you to focus your thoughts, highlight areas which you will have to explore during the interview and identify questions you will need to ask. Even if, for example, the instructions are as brief as saying that the client wants to make a will this should alert you to the fact that as well as obtaining instructions on the terms of the will you will need to find out about the client's assets, their family situation (including any plans to marry/enter a civil partnership), whether there is an existing will etc. and that you may have to explore issues as to capacity or duress.

Precisely how much information is given about the detail of the client's case will vary. Even if you are provided with quite a lot of information, it is important not to pre-judge the matter. If you make incorrect assumptions based on the information you have at this stage the interview is likely to go off on a tangent with important issues being overlooked.

It is a good idea to make a note of the issues that you anticipate will have to be discussed which you can then use as a prompt during the interview. However, it is best to make a note of 'points to cover' rather than laboriously writing out longhand questions as the latter will both waste time and risk the interview becoming a formulaic reading out of a list of pre-prepared questions.

As part of the instructions, you may be provided with a document which forms part of the client's matter. In reading through the document, you can make a note, perhaps by marking up the document itself, of any elements which require clarification or further information from the client. You should examine the document with a critical eye. For example, if you are presented with a will, as well as familiarising yourself with its terms, you should be examining it to see whether there is anything on the face of the will to call its validity into question or cause a gift to fail. Note also any information given about the document for the purposes of the assessment. For example, if the instructions say that the signatures on the document are genuine, you can proceed on that basis.

The instructions may also indicate some particular questions or concerns that the client has. Needless to say, you will need to ensure that these are covered during the interview and addressed as part of your advice.

You will need to make a contemporaneous note during the interview. You can plan for this by using some of your preparation time to set out the structure for those notes, e.g. headings for each section of the notes with blank spaces in between to be completed during the interview. Your 'points to cover' (see above) can be slotted into the structure at an appropriate place. It is advisable for the structure of your contemporaneous notes to align with the structure of the full attendance note which you will make in the second part of the assessment (see **Chapter 5**).

4.4 The 'client'

Although the interview in the SQE2 assessments is a role-play, it is intended to be as authentic as possible. So, the assessor's brief will be to reflect how a 'real' client would approach the interview. In an ideal world every client would be placid, reasonable, sensible, ready and willing both to provide all the information you require and meekly accept the advice you have to give. In reality, whilst some clients fit that description perfectly, that is not always the case and therefore you cannot assume that it will be so in the SQE2 assessments.

You should be ready for the fact that in the SQE2 assessments the client may not behave precisely as you would wish. The possibilities are endless, but you may, for example, be faced with a client who is confrontational, verbose, unreasonable, nervous, reticent or unwilling to accept advice. You are expected to be able to deal with clients of all types and so you need to be sufficiently agile to adapt your approach and respond to the unique individual before you. So, for example, if the client has a tendency to ramble on about irrelevant matters you may need to adapt your questioning technique by taking a more proactive approach in order to keep the client on track.

You should also be ready for the possibility that your client may be in a vulnerable situation (see **3.2.2**). This may be obvious from the outset or emerge from the discussions during the interview. Some vulnerabilities can be addressed more easily, for example a solicitor should show a bereaved client empathy. Other vulnerabilities may need more practical adjustments and you will need to be sensitive to this. For example, a client who is partially sighted might need correspondence and documents to be sent to them in large font, or a client with literacy difficulties might need documents read to them.

If you have concerns that your client might be vulnerable you may choose to ask the client at the outset. The following wording could be adapted:

> Please let me know if you have any accessibility needs, preferences or concerns about today's interview and how I can support you going forward.

4.5 The interview

The following is a review of the stages of the suggested interviewing model applicable to any client first interview (see **3.7**). Specific reference is also made to the SQE2 assessments as appropriate.

A first interview with a client is often the most difficult type of interview to conduct because there is a good deal to cover. The stages of the model as described can be adapted for an interview with an existing client.

Your demeanour during the SQE2 assessments should be the same as it would be when conducting an interview in practice: calm, professional and objective throughout. Remember that one of the criteria that you will be assessed against is your ability to conduct yourself 'in a professional manner and treat the client with courtesy, respect and politeness including respecting diversity where relevant'.

4.5.1 Greeting

The importance of a warm and friendly greeting cannot be over-emphasised. Some of the points that follow are simply common courtesy and may seem obvious, but they are extremely important.

A client will form an impression of their solicitor as soon as they meet. A solicitor should therefore do everything possible to ensure that this impression is favourable, and that the client is made to feel welcome, comfortable and relaxed.

It is important to greet a client by making eye contact and addressing them by name. The solicitor should also introduce themself by name and explain their status within the firm. For example:

Good morning Mr Brown. My name is Alex West and I am a solicitor with the firm.

In the SQE2 assessments you will have been given the client's name in the instructions. It is obviously important to make a mental note of it during your preparation time.

The conventional greeting in a business context also involves shaking hands. However, this is by no means essential, and indeed factors such as cultural differences may render it wholly inappropriate. A professional, confident greeting can be achieved without the need to shake hands. The shaking of hands was obviously abandoned during the coronavirus crisis. Even in a post-pandemic world it is likely that many people will be reluctant to shake hands. The important point is that you should respect the sensitivities of others and protect your own.

Many clients do not regularly consult solicitors. When they do have cause to do so, it is likely to be at a time when they are experiencing a very difficult situation. The prospect of meeting a solicitor may be quite daunting and add to their already stressful state of mind. Friendly conversation about such things as the weather or the client's journey may help put a client at ease.

In the SQE2 assessments engaging in a little friendly conversation presents a good opportunity for you to begin to connect with the client. However, to achieve this it is important that the conversation comes across as genuine and is appropriate to the client's circumstances. For example, 'Have you been enjoying all this fantastic weather that we've been having recently?' might be an appropriate opening for a client who is coming to see you because they are buying a property but is unlikely to be so for a client who is coming to see you as a result of a recent bereavement. It may be necessary for you to manage the conversation. For example, if the client responds to a benign enquiry about their journey with a lengthy tirade detailing how terrible an experience it was, it may be necessary for you to sensitively apply a break and move the client on to the substance of the interview, such as, 'That does sound awful. We can certainly arrange any future meetings so that it gives you plenty of time to do the school run first...'.

Recent years have seen a rise in the number of client meetings being undertaken using virtual means, and of course they became the only method of conducting business during the pandemic. Conducting client interviews using video links is likely to continue to be a significant feature of a solicitor's practice in the future. Many of the points made above will still apply when greeting a client in a virtual meeting. It is still necessary to create a first impression that establishes rapport with the client and appears professional and confident. Greeting the client, establishing good eye contact and initiating conversation designed to put them at ease are, if anything, even more important when not meeting a client in person.

After the greeting, it is a matter of judgment how quickly the solicitor proceeds to the business at hand, but most clients will have been rehearsing what they wish to say and will be ready to begin at once. With only 25 minutes to conduct the interview in the SQE2 assessments it is vital not to waste time.

4.5.2 Opening

It can be useful to briefly address some preliminary points before the interview gets fully underway. This stage is characterised in the main by the solicitor imparting information to the client. Where it is necessary to ask questions, it is important to use only closed questions. To enable the solicitor to keep control of the interview, the client should not perceive any question as an invitation to launch into their reason for making the appointment until the solicitor is ready for them to do so.

In practice, when arranging the appointment for the interview, a client will have given some indication of the general nature of the matter and the reason for seeking advice. This will also be the case in the SQE2 assessments. Nevertheless, ambiguities may still arise. 'I want to see a solicitor about a will' may not necessarily mean that a client wishes to make a will; they may want to challenge the validity of a will. It is therefore sensible to ask your client to confirm your understanding of the reason for the visit before encouraging them to launch into a lengthy account of the facts. This should be a quick check by way of a closed question to avoid them thinking they are being invited to fully explain the reason for their visit.

Once this confirmation has been obtained, there are a few matters which can usefully be dealt with before the interview proceeds further.

- **The conduct of the interview**

    In the SQE2 assessments it makes sense to start by saying a little about how you propose to conduct the interview. It does not need to be more than, for example:

    First, I'll ask you to explain why you have come to see me. Then I will need to ask you some questions and make some notes. From time to time, I may need to stop you or ask you to repeat something just so that I can be sure that I am understanding everything correctly. Finally, when I have got the complete picture, I shall explain what your legal position is and between us, we can then decide what, if anything, needs to happen next.

    This helps to manage the client's expectations. It also enables you to take control of the interview from the outset and, if necessary, keep the client on track.

- **Checks and client care**

    In legal practice there are a number of checks and client care matters which need to be addressed at or before a first interview (see **3.6.2** and **3.6.6**). Whilst there is no absolute rule as to when these should be addressed during the interview, some are best dealt with at the beginning. These are mentioned here for completeness. Whether you will be required to deal with all or any of them in the SQE2 assessments will depend in the first instance on the scenario. However, you must check your instructions carefully as there may be a specific direction to the effect that such matters do not need to be addressed.

    o   Due diligence
        In practice the necessary checks are best dealt with in advance of the first meeting. The Money Laundering, Terrorist Financing and Transfer of Funds (Information on the Payer) Regulations 2017 require a solicitor to carry out due diligence in respect of their clients. In other words, to be satisfied that the client is who they claim to be. In most cases this requires the client to produce two original documents, one of which provides photographic evidence of the client's identity and the other confirms the client's address. Examples of acceptable documents include a passport, driving licence, recent utility bill and recent bank statement (see The University of Law SQE1 manual *Legal Services*).

    o   The cost of the interview
        A solicitor must obviously comply with the requirements of professional conduct. In particular the need to ensure that a client is given the best information possible, both at the time of engagement and as the matter progresses, about the likely overall cost of their matter (Paragraph 8.7 SRA Code of Conduct for Solicitors, RELs and RFLs) (see The University of Law SQE1 manual *Ethics and Professional Conduct*).
        Clients naturally tend to be concerned about the cost of the interview and, indeed, of the whole matter. Until the complete picture has been obtained, it is usually difficult to say anything meaningful about the latter, and this must therefore be postponed until later stages of the interview. However, the preliminaries stage of the interview is a good time to explain to a client how the firm will charge for the interview itself. This may be by reference to an hourly charging rate or a fixed fee. Even if the firm's policy is to provide the initial interview free of charge, it will be reassuring for a client if this is confirmed early on in the interview. In legal practice, if relevant, it may also be necessary to establish whether a client will be paying the costs or if there is an external source of funding, such as Legal Aid or legal expenses insurance.

    o   Complaints

Paragraphs 8.3 and 8.4 SRA Code of Conduct for Solicitors, RELs and RFLs requires that a client be given information in writing about their right to complain and how to complain (see The University of Law SQE1 manual *Ethics and Professional Conduct*). Within the constraints of the SQE assessments you are unlikely to have time to address a complaints procedure in any detail. A sensible approach would therefore be to say that such a procedure exists and that the detail will be confirmed in writing after the meeting.

4.5.3   Listening/obtaining the relevant information

This stage involves the client giving an account of the matter with as little interruption from the solicitor as possible. It is therefore characterised by the client talking and the solicitor listening, observing the client's body language (see **2.10.2**) and encouraging the client to continue. The objective during this stage and the next (filling in the detail) is to obtain all relevant information from the client and to fully understand the client's concerns.

In legal practice this stage usually begins with the solicitor encouraging the client to give an account of the matter in their own words. There is no set form of wording.

Consider the impact on the client of the following choice of words and expressions:

'So, where shall we start?' (Does not inspire confidence)

'What's the problem, then?' (There may not be a 'problem')

'Thank you for sending me the documentation ... It seems to me ...' (Over-directional – premature diagnosis)

'Things don't look too good, do they?' (Prematurely pessimistic – provokes anxiety)

'Don't worry, we'll sort this out for you.' (Prematurely optimistic – raises expectations)

'This is the one, I think. Now then, where are we? ... Let me see ... dah dah dah dah ... Oh yes that's right, this is an Inheritance Act case, isn't it?' (Disorganised – unprepared – confusing use of jargon)

Clearly, therefore, in the SQE2 assessments you must give very careful thought to the form of words which you use to invite your client to begin this process. The question that you pose will be influenced by how much information you have been given about the client's matter in the instructions. For example, if your client wishes to make a will, saying 'Could you now give me some general background information?' is too vague to indicate what sort of information you require. A more focused form of words would be, 'Perhaps you could start by explaining what you would like your will to deal with'.

During the first part of this stage of the interview you should concentrate on listening and confine questions to open questions which will encourage your client to continue the narrative. As you begin to build up a fuller picture of the matter, it is important that your questions try to follow the client's train of thought. Your open questions should encourage the client to expand on a particular topic or, as appropriate, to move on to a different aspect. It is important to avoid jumping around topics, asking questions as they come to mind or following a generic list of pre-prepared questions. Approaching questioning in a random or indiscriminate manner may hinder building up a clear picture of a client's matter and is likely to cause a client to omit facts from their explanation. A good questioning technique should be logical and should facilitate a client's recall and thought processes.

At this stage of the interview, you will be obtaining the facts of the case, but it is equally important to establish your client's thoughts and feelings about the situation. You may need to prompt your client by asking questions along the lines of, 'it would be helpful if you could let me know any particular concerns which you have' and 'do you foresee any problems?' Such questions will allow you to begin to identify your client's particular needs and anxieties.

There will be opportunity in the next stage of the interview to clarify points of detail. You should therefore resist any temptation to do so at this stage, because a series of closed questions can easily destroy your client's concentration. For the same reason, making written notes should, if possible, be restricted to what can be written without interrupting your client's narrative flow.

This comparatively passive role enables you to maintain eye contact with your client and to observe their general demeanour and manner of delivery. This is very helpful in building rapport with your client and in picking up body language signals about your client's feelings.

4.5.4   Filling in the detail

In this stage of the interview the solicitor adopts a more active role to ensure that a complete and accurate picture is obtained and recorded. This stage is therefore characterised by the solicitor questioning the client and taking notes of what the client says. The objective is for the solicitor to obtain a full and accurate understanding and to record the relevant facts and the client's wishes and objectives.

It is not usually possible to give a client effective advice immediately after they have completed their account of the matter in the 'Listening/obtaining the relevant information' stage. In most cases, it will be necessary to ask a client to fill gaps or explain discrepancies in the narrative or to supply information which they had not considered to be relevant. For example, a client who wants to know how much inheritance tax is payable on an estate may well have given a full account of the assets but is unlikely to have appreciated that a key piece of information in answering that question is whether the deceased made any lifetime gifts. This stage of the interview is the place to address such gaps.

During this stage of the interview in the SQE2 assessments you should assume a more directive role. You will also need to take written notes and check that you have correctly understood what your client has said.

Questioning skills become more important although, even at this stage, it is generally best to use the T-funnel approach (see **3.5.2.2**). In other words, see what information can be elicited in response to open questions before pinning down a client with more specific closed questions. It may be necessary to use some clarifying and probing techniques to jog your client's memory or to explore discrepancies or weaknesses in your client's version of events.

It may also be necessary to examine documents handed over by your client in the course of the interview. You should not attempt to read a document at the same time as your client is speaking. Not only might this hinder rapport, but it is very difficult to read and listen at the same time. Explain to your client that you need a few moments to read the document so that there is a 'comfortable' silence while you are reading.

In the SQE2 assessments your client will have a full 'back story'. It will not be necessary for you to extract every point of detail. However, you will obviously need to use listening and questioning techniques to obtain enough information to understand the client's position and concerns and to provide preliminary advice appropriately. Remember that one of the criteria you will be assessed against is your ability to 'listen to the client and use questioning effectively to enable the client to tell [you] what is important to them'.

4.5.5   Advising

This stage involves supplying the information which the client needs in order to understand their legal position and, if necessary, to make decisions and give the solicitor instructions for further action. In legal practice this stage therefore typically takes the form of the solicitor analysing and explaining the client's position, explaining the range of options open to the client and then engaging in a dialogue to make necessary decisions and to agree a plan of action.

Paragraph 8.6 SRA Code of Conduct for Solicitors, RELs and RFLs requires that clients should be in a position to make informed decisions about the services they need, how their matter will be handled and the options available to them. At this stage of the interview the solicitor should explain the relevant issues, the different ways in which the matter could progress and any likely complications as well as the solicitor's role and responsibilities and the services the firm can or cannot provide.

In the SQE2 assessments the specific points to be covered at this stage will be dictated by the nature of the client's instructions. However, in essence you may need to do *one or more* of the following:

- explain your client's current legal position;
- address any specific questions or concerns raised by your client;
- discuss the main options (both legal and non-legal) for resolving the issues or achieving your client's objectives;
- outline procedural or transactional steps;
- help your client to reach a decision/give instructions; and
- agree a plan of action.

4.5.5.1 Explaining the legal position

In legal practice it is often not possible to give absolute and definitive advice at a first client interview. Much will depend on how the matter progresses or the obtaining of further evidence/information. However, it will usually be possible to provide sufficient preliminary advice to enable a client to have a broad understanding of their current legal position and the way forward.

The SQE2 assessments mirrors practice in this regard. The SRA Assessment Specification states that you will not be expected to provide detailed advice. Instead, you can conduct the interview on the basis that you will be advising the client in detail at a later date. However, you will need to give sufficient preliminary advice and to address enough of your client's concerns to establish your client's trust and confidence.

You should not be tempted into giving definitive advice, even if pressed to do so by your client, unless it is clearly justified on the facts. You may need to explain to your client why your advice must be limited at this stage, for example because your full advice must await further information or a thorough review of the evidence. It is equally important not to speculate on what facts may come to light or how the situation might develop. Instead, you should base your advice on the facts before you, explain to the client that this is the case and warn the client that your advice may have to change if further information is discovered.

It is essential to package your advice in a way that allows your client to follow your line of reasoning and understand it. Remember that one of the criteria that you will be assessed against is your ability to communicate and explain in a way that is suitable for your client to understand. Your client's legal position should be explained in clear, simple and comprehensible language. Therefore, it is important to avoid jargon. In preparing to conduct the interview, it is a good idea to give conscious thought to the best way of explaining the likely relevant issues to a lay client; for example, the distinction between joint tenants and tenants in common or the effect of a contingent interest. There is no need to use statute names, section numbers or case names; in fact, such details are undesirable because, rather than impressing a client, they only serve to confuse or overload a client with unnecessary details.

Clarity of advice also involves trying to structure your advice so that it is given to a client in an order that is easy to follow. For example, it would probably make more sense to explain the nature of the breach of covenant first, before moving on to consider the available remedies.

It is important to demonstrate that you have understood the problem from the client's perspective. A client's primary concern will be to know how the law impacts on their personal situation, rather than receiving a generic description of the law. For example, a client who wants to know how much capital gains tax will be payable on their property sale, will be more interested in a best estimate of the final figure, than in a detailed account of the statutory steps that must be applied in order to carry out the calculation.

Not every client's problem can be solved easily, and indeed some cannot be solved at all. It will therefore sometimes be necessary for you to impart 'bad news' or advice which it may be difficult for your client to face. For example, the lack of provision for cohabitants is a straightforward feature of the intestacy rules. However, explaining this to the intestate's lifelong partner will require particular care and sensitivity. It would be wholly inappropriate, for example, to fall back on standard wording which might suffice in other circumstances, such as 'under the rules an estate passes to the deceased's family'.

4.5.5.2 Addressing particular issues

At the time of making the appointment or during the course of the earlier stages of the interview itself it is highly likely that a client will raise particular questions or concerns about their legal position. For example, a client may be seeking advice on how their late father's estate will pass under the intestacy rules but has a particular concern about whether the client's elderly mother can be spared from being involved in the administration of the estate.

This possibility is anticipated in the SRA Assessment Specification which states that the email which forms your instructions for the interview may 'indicate specific legal issues which candidates should have particular regard to in the interview and the subsequent attendance note/case analysis'. It is therefore important to note any such issues, explore them with the client and address them as part of your advice.

4.5.5.3 Outlining procedural or transactional steps

The nature of a client's matter may be such that the solicitor needs to make them aware of the steps that need to be followed to achieve their desired outcome. In doing so the solicitor should also flag up the possibility of potential problems or complications, which may mean that the process takes longer than expected or may lead to the solicitor having to follow a different course. Managing a client's expectations in this way should ensure that they feel more closely involved with the matter, and less likely to believe that things are going wrong or that the solicitor has made a mistake in their handling of the case.

The subject matter of the SQE2 assessments is such that procedural or transactional issues may arise. In accordance with the SRA Assessment Specification, you will not be required to give detailed advice. However, in an appropriate case it may be necessary, for example, to outline the basic steps in a conveyancing transaction or the key stages in the administration of an estate.

4.5.5.4 Discussing the options

For some clients an explanation of the legal position is a precursor to discussing the courses of action available to them. The explanation of the law serves to set the available options in context. Such clients need to be given a clear explanation of what realistic options are open to them in order to achieve their desired objectives or resolve the issues. Managing a client's expectations now can reduce the risk of dissatisfaction and complaint later on in the solicitor/client relationship. An explanation of the options must be supported by thorough discussion with the client of the relative merits of each option.

Clearly, the strength of the legal aspects of the case will influence a discussion of the client's options, but there are other factors which will have an impact on a client's decision. In particular, a client's decision as to which option to pursue may be influenced by the possible timeframe involved, the level of costs, the commercial risks and personal factors such as emotion, health, family relationships, professional embarrassment and possible adverse publicity. For example, litigation is not only emotionally stressful, costly and time-consuming, it can be severely disruptive to home and work life if a client and others have to spend days at court waiting to give evidence. It may make commercial sense for a client to do nothing about a particular issue because, despite any injustice, it is not economically worthwhile. It may be that cash flow will prevent the taking of a particular course of action. Equally, it may be necessary to take action, despite the costs, for example, to preserve the rights of children or protect a vulnerable person.

The subjects which form the basis of the SQE2 assessments do not naturally lend themselves to the client being faced with a range of options as to how to take the matter forward. However, it is not impossible that some discussion of options will be necessary. For example, a client who wants to make a family provision claim essentially is faced with the choice of litigation or negotiation (either direct or through solicitors). Again, in accordance with the SRA Assessment Specification, detailed advice is not required, but it would be appropriate to, say, mention the benefits of negotiation over litigation in terms of reducing costs, stress and family disharmony (see The University of Law manual *Written Skills for Lawyers*, Chapter 3).

4.5.5.5 Helping the client to make a decision

It is sometimes the case that the culmination of a first interview is for the client to make a fundamental decision about the case itself or how the matter is to proceed. All major decisions concerning the case or transaction are for the client to make. However, opinion is divided on how far the solicitor may recommend a course of action for the client. The non-directive school suggests that a solicitor should only present the options and leave it entirely to the client to decide which to follow. The directive school involves the solicitor in taking greater control of the decision-making process. In practice a combination of each approach is appropriate in most cases. The solicitor should explain the realistic options to a client and explore the positive and negative consequences of each. Provided the client actively participates in this explorative discussion and the solicitor actively seeks the client's views and preferences, the decision will often be clear.

Decision-making will not be a feature of every first interview. For example, if a client wants advice on how an estate will be distributed then, in the absence of a dispute, there will be no decision as such for the client to make. Furthermore, even if a decision is required, the client may need time after the interview to consider their position.

4.5.5.6 Agreeing a future plan of action

During a first interview it will sometimes be necessary to agree a more detailed plan of action, i.e. to decide what is the best way of carrying out the course of action which has been agreed. For example, if a client has decided to try to settle a matter by agreement rather than go to court, it will still need to agree:

- whether to approach the other party immediately or await their next move; and

- whether any first approach should be made by the solicitor or the client, and if so:

  o whether it should be by letter, telephone or in person
  o what (if any) opening offer should be made and how far the client is prepared to go in order to settle.

In bringing the advising stage of the interview to a close, you should ensure that everything has been discussed to your client's satisfaction. A form of wording could be as follows: 'Can

I just check whether you clearly understand your position or if there is anything you would like me to clarify.'

4.5.6 Closing

Once the issues have been discussed and the client has decided what, if anything, needs to be done or has decided to go away and consider their options more carefully, there are still a number of matters which may still need to be dealt with before bringing an interview to a conclusion. Not all of these matters will need to be covered in the SQE2 assessments. They are set out here for completeness, but you will need to be selective depending on the facts of the case.

In essence, the aim of the closing stage of an interview in practice is to ensure that both solicitor and client leave the interview being clear as to what will happen next, how quickly the matter will be resolved and what it will all cost.

4.5.6.1 Next steps/follow-up tasks

During the interview, it is essential for the solicitor to establish exactly what, if anything, the client is instructing them to do. When dealing with a new client, especially one who is not used to consulting solicitors, the solicitor should explain their role and the services the firm provides.

In the SQE2 assessments, even though the next steps are likely to have been mentioned earlier, in the closing stages of the interview, it is helpful to summarise what steps you have agreed to take and when you will take them. The steps will vary from case to case but might involve carrying out searches on a property, obtaining a valuation of assets, drafting a document or writing an offer of settlement.

In most cases, it is appropriate to write a follow-up letter to a client summarising what has been discussed and agreed. Telling a client that you intend to do this is obviously reassuring.

If you have not already done so, now is a good time to establish whether your client has any particular needs or preferences in terms of communication. You should discuss the best form of communicating with them, be it by email, letter or phone call. For example, a client may be worried about the privacy issues associated with emails or a partially sighted client may need letters to be typed in large font. It is essential to check that you have an accurate note of your client's address, telephone number and email address. Remember to confirm to which address they wish correspondence to be sent. This may be relevant if, for example, a client is involved in a family dispute when they may prefer correspondence not to be sent to their home address.

You should also remind your client of any action that they have agreed to take. This might include supplying information or documents which were not available during the interview or thinking about the advice or discussing their options with others and contacting you once a decision has been reached. If there is nothing you need your client to do at this stage, it is useful to state this clearly.

4.5.6.2 Alternative contact

If someone else at the firm is to have overall supervision of the matter it can be useful at this point to provide a client with their name together with any appropriate alternative contact who a client can speak to if you are not available, or if they have any complaint. Alternatively, these can be left to a follow-up letter or client information sheet.

4.5.6.3 Time frame

Some clients only require advice on their current legal position. However, if the matter is to progress in some way, the solicitor should be given some indication of how long it will take to complete. This should help manage a client's expectations and minimise the risk of complaints about delays in situations where the outcome is likely to take some time to attain. Sometimes an estimate is quite easy to give:

> As the terms are quite straightforward, I shall be able to send you a draft of the will by the end of the week. Then, if you're happy with it, it should be possible to finalise it and have it ready for you to execute sometime during next week.

In other cases, particularly where court proceedings are a possibility, it may be impossible to do no more than give a very broad estimate because future developments will to a large extent be unpredictable and outside the solicitor's control. Even in these situations, the solicitor should try to give some indication of time frame, even if it is only to indicate that the matter could potentially take years rather than months.

4.5.6.4 Estimating the costs of the matter/method of charging

If you are required to deal with costs in the SQE2 assessments, you may need revisit the subject in the closing stages of the interview.

In practice, costs will usually have been discussed during the course of the interview. It will usually be possible to explain early in the interview how the interview itself is to be paid for, but it is seldom possible at that stage to discuss the likely cost of the matter itself. When discussing any options available to the client there should have been some analysis of the costs implications.

In closing the interview, it is helpful for the solicitor to give a summary of the position as to costs to ensure that the client understands clearly the potential costs they are facing. Information on costs, together with details of possible disbursements (charges or fees that will be incurred in carrying out the legal work which are not included in the firm's charging rate, such as the payment of stamp duty land tax), should also be summarised as part of the closing stage of the interview.

Paragraph 8.7 SRA Code of Conduct for Solicitors, RELs and RFLs requires that a client is given the best possible information on the likely overall costs of the matter. For the solicitor, deciding just what information they can reliably give a client at this stage can be a particularly tricky aspect of client care.

In some cases, commonly domestic conveyancing and simple will drafting, the firm may agree a fixed fee for handling a client's matter. The agreed fee should have been mentioned early on in the interview. During the closing stage, having received detailed instructions and not having found any unforeseen complications, it is appropriate to confirm the agreed fee.

In other cases, firms will calculate their bill by using an hourly charging rate and so the likely costs of the matter will involve the solicitor estimating how much time will be involved in handling the matter. As a bare minimum, a client should be told the relevant hourly charging rate coupled with a realistic estimate of the time to be charged.

However, in many cases, it will be necessary for the solicitor to make it clear to a client that only a rough estimate of the total cost can be given (or perhaps a range of possible costs) because of the uncertainty as to how much work may need to be undertaken and the time it may take. For example, if protracted negotiations are going to be necessary, the solicitor will be less certain as to the amount of time that will be involved in completing the matter:

> It is difficult to estimate how much of my time will be taken up during the negotiations, and so it is impossible to give you a precise estimate of the overall costs. It may well amount to over £1,000 but I will report to you regularly about the costs as the matter progresses.

There are situations, particularly those involving potential litigation, where it may not be possible to give a realistic overall cost of the matter. In such cases, the solicitor should explain this to the client and instead give the best information possible about the cost of the next stage of the matter. For example, the solicitor might advise the client as follows:

It is impossible, at this stage, for me to give a realistic estimate of the costs that will be involved. We have agreed that the next step will be for me to instruct a barrister to provide an opinion. In my experience, the cost of my time in preparing the instructions to the barrister and the barrister's fees in providing such an opinion is likely to be in the region of £2,000 plus VAT. Before instructing the barrister, I will need you to provide me with £1,000 which I will hold pending payment of the costs I incur on your account. Once we have the opinion, we can meet again to discuss how you wish to proceed. I will, at that time, be in a better position to advise you further as to the likely costs.

In all cases when the solicitor is giving an estimate of costs, it may also be appropriate to offer assurances to the client: reassurance that the solicitor will keep them informed regularly as to how the costs are mounting during the matter; or perhaps agreeing a ceiling figure for costs, with their agreement being needed before costs beyond this figure are incurred. The client should be reassured that detailed information relating to costs will be confirmed in the follow-up letter.

4.5.6.5 Next contact

Where the client's instructions are going to be ongoing it can be helpful to avoid confusion by the solicitor explaining who is to make the next contact, whether another face-to-face meeting will be necessary and (if so) why and who will organise it.

4.5.6.6 Parting

In practice, when an interview is over, the solicitor would accompany the client back to the reception area or to the exit. The practicalities of the SQE2 assessments means that you may need to 'signal' the end of the interview, perhaps by standing (as if to show your client out), thanking your client for their time and, if appropriate offering some words of reassurance. The parting should be friendly and courteous.

4.6 Trust and confidence

The SRA Assessment Specification begins and ends with the concept of trust and confidence:

> In the interview candidates should aim to *win the client's trust and confidence*... to give enough preliminary advice and to address enough of the client's concerns to *establish the client's trust and confidence* [emphasis added].

Added to which, having an effective relationship with the client 'so as to *build trust and confidence*' [emphasis added] is one of the criteria against which you will be assessed.

It is easy to see that gaining trust and confidence must be a key aim when conducting the interview in the SQE2 assessments, but rather more difficult to describe precisely what 'trust and confidence' looks like or how to attain it.

Having trust and confidence means that the client will be assured that their case will be dealt with properly; they will be more likely to be accepting of your advice. If a client has trust and confidence in you, they will want you to act for them, be willing to instruct your firm on other matters and recommend you to their family and friends. A client's 'trust and confidence' is not guaranteed, rather it has to be earned. It is not gained at a single point in the interview but is capable of being lost at any stage.

Establishing trust and confidence begins as you make an initial connection with the client and develops as you create a professional rapport. A whole variety of factors contribute to it: how you present yourself (professional, confident etc.); putting the client at ease from the outset; how you conduct the interview; how the client feels about the process (demonstrating that you are listening, showing empathy, understanding the issues from the client's perspective).

4.7   Ethics and professional conduct issues

Ethics and professional conduct issues will not arise in every SQE2 assessment scenario. Your task is to identify when they do and to 'exercise judgment to resolve them honestly and with integrity'.

Ethics and professional conduct issues can arise in an Interviewing context in a variety of ways. A solicitor may be asked by a client to advise someone else involved in the case or transaction (such as for seller and buyer, for joint buyers or for borrower and lender) and so it will be necessary to consider whether doing so would give rise to a conflict of interest; a solicitor may be asked to draw up a will including a gift to the solicitor which may create an own interest conflict; a client may purport to give instructions on a joint basis in which case the solicitor will need to be satisfied that the client has authority to do so (see The University of Law manual *Ethics and Professional Conduct*).

As noted at **3.6.2** and **3.6.6** there are various checks to be carried out when instructed by a client and certain client care information to be given to a client 'at the time of engagement'. In the SQE2 assessments your instructions may state that you are not required to deal with such matters. However, if this is not the case you will have to address them briefly – see **4.5.2**.

4.8   Negotiation

The SQE2 Interviewing assessments may include negotiation. You should therefore be prepared to identify and advise upon negotiation as a possible option for finding a solution to the client's case and/or formulate a proposal for settlement or a strategy for negotiation (see The University of Law manual *Written Skills for Lawyers*, Chapter 3).

4.9   Contemporaneous notes

In the SQE2 assessments, just as in practice, you will need to make a contemporaneous note of the interview. The purpose of the contemporaneous note is to enable you to write a full attendance after the interview in the second part of the assessment.

It will be helpful for you if your contemporaneous note is clear, legible, comprehensible and follows the same structure as you intend to use for your full attendance note. Ensuring that your contemporaneous note meets these requirements is essential if you intend to cross-refer to it in your full attendance note (see **5.6**). If you intend to cross-refer, you should also make sure that there is some means to enable you to do so, for example, by using page or paragraph numbers.

In terms of the mechanics of taking notes during the interview there is obviously a tightrope to be walked between writing down enough to enable you to complete the full attendance note, and not writing so much that you interrupt the flow of the interview or run out of time.

4.10   Time management

At first sight, 25 minutes seems a short amount of time in which to conduct an interview. However, the SQE2 assessments will have been designed so as to be capable of successful completion within that time.

The explanation of the stages of the suggested interviewing model above is lengthy and may seem daunting. However, the explanation is deliberately comprehensive. It is important to remember that not every element will need to be covered in respect of the scenario that you will face in the SQE2 assessments. Additionally, you should note that stages which have been described at length above can be dealt with quickly in the interview. For example, checking the reason for the client's visit in the preliminaries stage will take a matter of seconds to complete in the SQE2 assessment itself.

All that having been said, time management is important. In the SQE2 assessments you will need to keep an eye on the clock and make sure that you are able to finish in time. The time limit will be rigidly enforced and so the interview will end whether you have finished all you wanted to say or not.

It is much better for you to keep control of the interview and bring it to a close yourself rather than have the interview brought to an abrupt end by the assessor. Therefore, if time is running out you may need to take steps to move the interview on to the closing stage by, for example, adapting the question that marks the end of the advising stage:

> Thank you. I think I have all the information that I need for now. Before we finish can I just check whether there is anything you would like me to clarify.

Even if time is so short that you realise that there are issues which you will not be able to explore, you should still bring the interview to a proper conclusion. Perhaps by adapting the above:

> Thank you. I think I have all the information that I need for now. If you decide to go ahead then we can arrange a further meeting to discuss the matter further. Now, before we finish can I just check whether there is anything you would like me to clarify.

Any outstanding issues should be noted in your full attendance note (see **Chapter 5**).

5 Attendance Note/Legal Analysis

SQE2 syllabus

This chapter will help you to achieve the SQE2 Assessment Objective of demonstrating that you are able to produce an attendance recording a client interview and initial legal analysis.

Learning outcomes

By the end of this chapter you will be able to

- plan a structured approach to recording a client interview; and

- produce an accurate and concise attendance note.

5.1 Introduction

The SQE2 Client Interviewing and Completion of Attendance Note/Legal Analysis assessments comprise two parts:

- conducting a client interview; and

- making a full attendance note.

General oral communication skills were considered in **Chapter 2** and **Chapter 3** explored client interviews in legal practice. This chapter looks at making an attendance note and considers the specific requirements of the SQE2 assessments. Conducting a client interview was dealt with in **Chapter 4**.

This chapter looks at:

- the purpose of an attendance note;

- the assessments;

- style;

- content;

- layout; and

- errors and omissions.

5.2 The purpose of an attendance note

During a client interview in legal practice the solicitor will have made a manuscript note of key points. Following the interview, the solicitor should make a full attendance note (usually typed) using the manuscript note as an aide memoire. Ideally this should be done immediately after the interview has taken place when the detail is fresh in the solicitor's mind. Any delay in writing up the note risks important points being forgotten or misremembered. An attendance note should be an accurate summary of what was discussed. It is not restricted to recording the facts of the matter and should incorporate the advice given, options discussed and action to be taken etc.

In legal practice an attendance note has several purposes:

- It is the starting point for the next steps in the case. It is usually necessary to send a letter after the interview confirming the client's instructions and the advice given by the solicitor. The attendance note will form the basis of that letter. Following the interview, the solicitor may have to draft a document or formulate a proposal for settlement; the attendance note should contain the information to enable this to be done without having to revert to the client asking for details provided during the interview to be repeated.

- No solicitor will be able to remember the facts of every one of their cases. As a client's matter progresses the solicitor will need to revisit the file. In doing so, the attendance note will serve to remind the solicitor of the facts, the client's objectives and the initial advice given.

- At some stage it may be necessary for a someone else in the firm to undertake work on the file or take over the conduct of the client's matter on a temporary or permanent basis. The attendance note should enable the colleague to become fully acquainted with the case and seamlessly undertake the work that needs to be done on the client's behalf. It would be professionally embarrassing and damaging to client confidence in the firm if the colleague had to contact the client and ask what the case is about.

- Something may go wrong with the client's matter and the solicitor accused of having given wrong or negligent advice. The attendance note should provide evidence of what was said and done at the interview (although it is still advisable to confirm the advice by letter).

- It may be that the solicitor's conduct is called into question for some reason. The attendance note should help the solicitor to demonstrate that they have complied with the SRA's regulatory requirements. Key such requirements include: 'You ensure that the service you provide to clients is competent and delivered in a timely manner' and 'You consider and take account of your client's attributes, needs and circumstances' (Paragraphs 3.2 and 3.4 SRA Code of Conduct for Solicitors, RELs and RFLs).

- It is a hard copy record of the time spent on the client's matter.

The notes taken during the interview, together with the full attendance note, the follow-up letter, copies of the client's proof of identity papers and the client care information sheet signed by the client during the interview should all be placed on the client's file.

5.3 The SQE2 assessments

5.3.1 Form

In the SQE2 assessments, immediately after conducting the client interview, candidates will be given 25 minutes in which to write up a full attendance note of the meeting. The attendance note must be handwritten (unless reasonable adjustments apply).

Candidates will sit a total of two Interviewing assessments in the practice areas below. Questions in these practice areas may draw on underlying black letter law in the Functioning Legal Knowledge shown in brackets next to each one:

- one in the context of Property Practice *(Land Law)*; and

- one in the context of Wills and Intestacy, Probate Administration and Practice *(Trusts)*.

The assessments may involve negotiation (see The University of Law manual *Written Skills for Lawyers*, Chapter 3). Remember that questions on ethics and professional conduct will be pervasive throughout SQE2.

(See the SRA website for the full syllabus.)

5.3.2 Criteria

In the SQE2 assessments candidates will be assessed against the following Assessment Criteria:

Skills

(1) Record all relevant information.

(2) Identify appropriate steps.

(3) Provide client-focused advice (i.e. advice which demonstrates an understanding of the problem from the client's point of view and what the client wants to achieve, not just from a legal perspective).

Application of law

(1) Apply the law correctly to the client's situation.

(2) Apply the law comprehensively to the client's situation, identifying any ethical and professional conduct issues and exercising judgment to resolve them honestly and with integrity.

Note that in this part of the assessment that candidates will be assessed on the application of law as well as their skills.

You can read more about the SQE assessments in **Chapter 1**. In the appendix to that chapter you can see how the Statement of Solicitor Competence applies to the skills of interviewing and making attendance notes.

5.4 Style

Given the practical constraints of the SQE2 assessments the attendance note must be handwritten (unless reasonable adjustments apply). You will therefore need to take care to ensure that it is clear, legible and comprehensible.

The primary purpose of the attendance note is to provide an orderly record of what was said at the interview. It is not the means by which the advice is conveyed to the client; that will already have happened during the course of the interview. The attendance note is therefore in a sense easier to write than, say, a letter of advice where language and tone are crucial elements in communicating effectively with the client. Nevertheless, it is still a professional piece of writing. You should pay attention to spelling, grammar and punctuation, and employ clear, precise language (see The University of Law SQE manual, *Written Skills for Lawyers*). Doing so will help to demonstrate the clarity of thought that you should aim to convey to the assessor.

With only 25 minutes available in the SQE2 assessment you will need to make the attendance note concise. The use of bullet points is acceptable, but they need to be employed with care. The danger with bullet points is that they are so brief that, whilst they can be understood by the writer, they are incomprehensible to the reader. So, if you decide to use bullet points you should ensure that they are sufficiently full so as to be understood by the assessor.

The attendance note can cross-refer to the contemporaneous note that you took during the interview (see **4.9**). You can obviously produce the attendance note 'from scratch' if you prefer, but given the time constraints, some cross referencing may be prudent in order to avoid duplication and to save time. If you decide to cross refer you will need to ensure that the format of the contemporaneous notes and the attendance note are aligned so that it is easy to look between documents. You will also need to incorporate some means for cross-referring such as page or paragraph numbering.

5.5 Content

The SRA Assessment Specification stipulates that a number of matters must be recorded in the attendance note:

* all relevant information obtained during the interview;

* an analysis of any legal issues that arise and the initial advice given;

* next steps to be taken by the solicitor;

* next steps to be taken by the client (if applicable);

* any ethical issues that arise and how they should be dealt with;

* options and strategies for negotiation (if applicable); and

* the advice given on any specific issues or questions raised.

5.6 Layout

There is no set or required form for an attendance note. In legal practice firms tend to have their own in-house style or template. In the SQE2 assessment you can present your attendance note in whatever form you choose. It should, however, be clear, logical and comprehensive and, of course, enable you to demonstrate that you have met the assessment criteria. The template below is merely a suggestion which can be adapted or discarded in meeting your own style and preferences.

Client:

Matter:

Fee earner:

Date/Time:

Time taken:

Details:

Facts/Concerns:

Advice:

Follow-up steps:

Most attendance notes have a heading containing some basis information about the interview. The precise content may vary, but the above is a typical example. The heading should be completed with the name of the client, a brief description of the matter, the name of the person conducting the interview, the date and time of day that the interview took place and the amount of time spent on the interview.

The body of the attendance note should follow a logical structure. It is best divided into separate sections with appropriate side-headings for clarity and to aid navigation around the content. The structure of the attendance note is unlikely to follow the chronology of the interview. The aim is to introduce order. For example, you may not have noted down the client's address until the closing stage of the interview, but it is more logical for the address to appear at the beginning of the attendance note.

Details

It is often convenient to gather together basic information about the client in one place at the beginning of the attendance note. The precise detail will vary depending on the nature of the matter, but will usually include full name and address, phone number, email address etc.

It may also be necessary to note down the details of others who are involved in the case and who will need to be contacted, e.g. a mortgage lender or the executors of the estate.

Facts/concerns

The Assessment Criteria requires all relevant information to be recorded. The important word in that sentence is 'relevant'. There is no need to write down everything that the client says, indeed you will not have time to do so. You should focus on the key information. By the same token, the record does not need to be verbatim and so you will need to summarise as appropriate.

The 'relevant information' is not restricted to facts. If the client has raised any particular concerns or wishes to achieve a specific objective these should also be noted.

Advice

The relevant legal issues should arise from the facts/concerns. Those legal issues should be noted together with the advice given and any options discussed. The focus should be on how the law applies to the facts of the case; in other words, how the law impacts on the client. If any particular queries or issues have been revealed in your instructions or emerge during the interview these must be addressed here.

It is in this section of the attendance note that you should demonstrate your ability to carry out legal analysis. The SQE2 Assessment Criteria require you to apply the law correctly and comprehensively to the client's situation. For an answer to be comprehensive, it must go further than noting the issues and provide a legally comprehensive analysis of those issues. This includes approaching the issues from the client's point of view and weighing the advantages and disadvantages of available options.

There is no need to separate the facts/concerns and advice in this way. Depending on the nature of the client's case it may be more logical to consider both together or to structure the note by reference to the client's objectives.

If the scenario raises professional conduct issues (see **4.7**) you may wish to address these under a separate heading.

Follow-up steps

The steps that need to be taken following the interview need to be noted. These are steps to be taken both by the solicitor and the client. The steps will vary from case to case. In most cases it will be necessary to write a follow-up letter; other steps might include the client bringing in some documentation, the solicitor drafting a document or contacting a third party.

5.7   Errors and omissions

It may be that when writing up the attendance note you realise that you did not deal with an important issue during the interview or said something in error. For example, you may have forgotten to ask about a key fact, made a mistake on the law, not advised on a particular issue or simply have run out of time. It goes without saying that the attendance note must be truthful and so matters which were not discussed at the interview cannot be presented in the attendance note as if they had. Such errors and omissions do sometimes happen in practice and would usually be dealt with, for example, by way of a further meeting or follow-up telephone call with the client. For the purposes of the assessment a reasonable approach would be to identify and explain the issue in the attendance note and set out what future action needs to be taken to enable it to be addressed.

6 Advocacy: Preparing for a Hearing

SQE2 syllabus

This chapter will help you to achieve the SQE2 Assessment Objective of demonstrating that you are able to conduct a piece of advocacy before a judge.

Learning outcomes

By the end of this chapter you should be able to prepare effectively for a hearing by:

- analysing the law and the facts;
- identifying strengths and weaknesses in the parties' cases;
- putting together submissions;
- preparing an advocacy plan; and
- identifying any ethical and professional conduct issues.

6.1 Introduction

What is advocacy? In its widest sense advocacy is the art of influencing outcomes. It is about convincing others: the art of persuasion. In this general sense, it is a valued accomplishment in many areas of life. This chapter is, however, concerned with the specialised meaning of the word as used by lawyers; in its legal context, advocacy is the skill of presenting legal argument to a court or tribunal. The person practising that skill is known as an advocate.

This chapter focuses on the preparation of the piece of advocacy which you will be required to carry out in the SQE2 assessments.

It looks at:

* the assessments;

* how to prepare;

* formulating your submissions; and

* ethical and professional conduct issues.

This chapter should be read in conjunction with **Chapter 2** on oral communication skills and **Chapter 7** which deals with the presentation of the piece of advocacy.

Chapter 8 contains a more detailed description of bail applications and pleas in mitigation in the context of a criminal case study. **Chapter 9** looks at interim applications in the civil courts and contains a case study for an application for summary judgment. This chapter cross refers to those case studies to illustrate good practice.

6.2 The SQE2 assessments

6.2.1 Form

In the SQE2 Advocacy assessments candidates will be given a case study on which they will conduct a piece of courtroom advocacy. An email will ask the candidate to conduct the advocacy and will tell them in which court they are appearing. Where relevant, candidates are also given a file of documents.

Candidates will sit two Advocacy assessments in the practice areas below. Questions in these practice areas may draw on underlying black letter law in the Functioning Legal Knowledge (FLK) shown in brackets next to each one:

* one in the context of Dispute Resolution *(Contract Law and Tort)*; and

* one in the context of Criminal Litigation *(Criminal Liability)*.

Remember that questions on ethics and professional conduct will be pervasive throughout SQE2.

(See the SRA website for the full syllabus.)

You will be given 45 minutes to prepare. You will then have 15 minutes to make your submissions to a judge who is present in the room. The judge will be played by a solicitor of England and Wales who will assess you both on skills and application of the law. You may be asked questions during the advocacy.

6.2.2 Criteria

In the SQE2 Advocacy assessments candidates will be assessed against the following Assessment Criteria:

Skills

(1) Use appropriate language and behaviour.

(2) Adopt a clear and logical structure.

(3) Present a persuasive argument.

(4) Interact with/engage the court appropriately.

(5) Include all key relevant facts.

Application of law

(1) Apply the law correctly to the client's situation.

(2) Apply the law comprehensively to the client's situation, identifying any ethical and professional conduct issues and exercising judgment to resolve them honestly and with integrity.

You can read more about the SQE2 oral assessments in **Chapter 1**. In the appendix to that chapter you can see how the Statement of Solicitor Competence (SoSC) applies to the skill of Advocacy; in particular you will see that B5 deals with 'undertaking effective spoken and written advocacy'.

6.2.3 In advance of the assessment

It is an obvious point, but a key aspect of preparing for the SQE2 is to ensure that you are confident in your knowledge of the law, as you will be assessed not only on your advocacy skills but also on your application of the law. Remember, however, that the level of knowledge required for the assessments is that of a Day One solicitor. If the piece of advocacy requires knowledge of an aspect of the law which a Day One solicitor would have to look up, this will be given to you in the assessments.

The subject matter of the SQE2 Advocacy assessments is restricted to the areas of Dispute Resolution and Criminal Litigation (see the SRA website for the full syllabus). You will therefore need to draw on the FLK you used in passing SQE1, both in these practice areas and the related black letter law. As you will know from SQE1, these subject areas are broad in themselves. Consequently, you will not be able to predict the content of the assessments with any certainty. You can, however, think about possible scenarios (such as a bail application or an application for summary judgment) and the legal principles that would apply to these.

6.3 Preparation

The SQE2 Advocacy assessments comprise two stages: preparation and presentation. Although you will be assessed on the quality of your advocacy you will see that more time (45 minutes) is allocated to preparation than to presentation (15 minutes). This, of course, reflects the reality of legal practice. An advocate will almost always spend longer preparing for a hearing than conducting it, but they will not have unlimited time available. This means that efficient preparation is essential, in legal practice and in the SQE2 assessments. How can you make the best use of the time available?

6.3.1 The initial read through

The starting point, in the SQE2 assessments as in legal practice, will be your instructions. You will be given a case study upon which you will conduct a piece of courtroom advocacy. You should, of course, start by reading through the information provided which will comprise an email asking you to conduct the advocacy and giving you the details of the court and, where appropriate, a file of documents.

You will want to answer some key questions straightaway, which will include:

- Which party do I represent? [Prosecution or defence? Claimant or defendant? Applicant or respondent?]

- What type of hearing is this? [Bail application? Application for summary judgment?]

- Which court will I be appearing in? [High Court? County Court? Magistrates' court?]

- Which issues have I been instructed to deal with?

- Are there any issues (such as costs) which I have been instructed to ignore?

- Do any ethical or professional conduct issues arise?

- What is the story?

Remember that you may be instructed to deal with more than one issue at the hearing. So, in a criminal case, you may be asked to make submissions on allocation and then to address the court on pre-trial issues. In a civil case you may be asked to deal with different procedural issues arising from the same claim.

6.3.2 Analysis

Having familiarised yourself with the documents and the story the next step in your preparation process is to carry out your analysis. You might find it helpful to approach this in the order below:

- the law

- the facts

- identify any gaps and inconsistencies in the facts

- link the facts to the law

- identify any strengths and weaknesses

- structure submissions

6.3.3 The law

Your first task is to identify the legal basis of the piece of advocacy and the relevant legal principles. In the assessments you may be provided with some law (such as the sentencing guidelines for a bail application). Remember that it may not all be relevant to your piece of advocacy. You should scan this, flagging and highlighting the points to which you may want to refer if possible.

You are unlikely to be provided with all the law which you require and will need to remember some of the legal and procedural rules which you have studied. In a civil case the legal basis of the piece of advocacy is likely to be the Civil Procedure Rules (CPR). By analogy with SQE1 you should not usually be required to cite specific provisions from the CPR. However, by way of example, if the piece of advocacy is a summary judgment application you should be able to recall the relevant test, which is that the court may give summary judgment against the defendant on the whole of a claim or particular issue if:

(a) it considers that the defendant has no real prospect of successfully defending the claim or issue; and

(b) there is no other compelling reason why the case or issue should be disposed of at a trial.

It is important to consider whether the grounds for a particular application are mandatory or discretionary. You will recall that a ground is mandatory if it is something which the court must grant if it is made out. It is discretionary if the court has a choice. For example, the court must set aside judgment in default if it has been wrongly entered. Otherwise, the court may set it aside if one of the relevant conditions is satisfied [by way of information this is CPR13]. If the ground is a discretionary one, the advocate's role is to try to persuade the court to exercise its discretion in the client's favour.

In the SQE2 assessments, by analogy with SQE1, you should not be required to recall specific case names, but you may be provided with a case (or an extract from one) as part of the assessment materials. As in legal practice, you will need to consider whether the case supports or detracts from your client's position and prepare your arguments on this basis. You can highlight the similarities between the facts of the case and those of the case study or distinguish between them. Do not worry if the facts of a case supplied are not 'on all fours' with the facts of the case study: this will rarely be the case and the important task is to identify the legal principle which the case establishes and consider how this affects the case you are dealing with.

6.3.4 The facts

Next, you can turn your attention to the facts. Mastering these is an essential first step. Until this is done, it is impossible to analyse the strengths and weaknesses of the case or to present it effectively in court.

Where to start? You may find it useful to prepare a brief chronology of key events. The chronology should end with the procedural steps taken in the claim so far. If the parties have given different versions of the facts, then you should flag this up on your chronology so that you are clear about where any conflicts of evidence are likely to arise. For example, there may be a dispute about exactly what was agreed during a telephone conversation between the parties.

Once you have got the events clear in your mind, you can begin to sift through the information to find facts to support the legal test or principle which you have identified. For example, if you are looking at the sentencing guidelines for a particular offence, you will be looking for facts which point to greater or lesser culpability, and for greater and lesser harm. So, for example, if the offence is assault occasioning actual bodily harm, one of the aggravating factors is a significant degree of premeditation. You will need to sift through the facts looking for evidence of this (if there is none, then the lack of it can indicate lower culpability).

Not all the facts you are given will be relevant, so do not assume that you will need to deploy every fact you have been given in your advocacy. Remember that you will only have 15 minutes to conduct the piece of advocacy in the assessment, so you should not waste time placing irrelevant material before the court.

6.3.5 Gaps and inconsistencies in the facts

Once you are clear about the facts you have been given, take a step back and consider whether anything is missing. One of the key skills of an advocate is to spot gaps and inconsistences in the information provided and to make use of these. In other words, when you are analysing the facts, pay attention to what is not there as well as what is. You are looking for situations where you might expect a person to say or do a particular thing – if their account of events is correct – but they do not do so. Remember that 'recognising inconsistencies and gaps in information' forms part of the SoSC (A5.b).

For example, in a civil claim a defendant might be complaining about shoddy work carried out to their house and refusing to pay the roofer, who has now brought a claim for payment of their outstanding bill. However, it appears from the documents that the claimant (the roofer) had been in regular contact with the defendant and that the defendant did not complain about the quality of the work on the roof when it was carried out, or at any time until the roofer chased for payment of the bill. If the work really was defective, one would expect the defendant to have complained straight away and to have mentioned this when they were in contact with the roofer.

In a criminal case, the defence might point to a lack of independent evidence to support the prosecution's version of events (as in the defence submissions on the bail application in the criminal case study, **Chapter 8**).

In both cases, these gaps can be deployed by the advocate to cast doubt on the account of events which is being presented to the court.

6.3.6 Linking the facts to the law

As you are analysing the facts you should begin to organise these so that they support your argument or position.

One way to do this is to bullet point the facts next to each legal point you intend to make. So, for example, taking the second limb of the test for summary judgment (see above) you might note:

LIMB 2 Some other compelling reason for trial

- *Wit 1 (sister) needs to give evidence about conversation*
- *Note of conversation not available- but might turn up*

Another approach is to list, in relation to each issue, which facts support your client's case, which undermine it, and which facts support and undermine your opponent's case.

6.3.7 Strengths and weaknesses

Having established a framework of the legal principles and the facts, you can now start to widen your analysis to identify the strengths and weaknesses of the parties' positions: see the SoSC (B5.h).

Clearly, an advocate should make the best use they can of any weaknesses in their opponent's case but what about weaknesses in their client's case? In the SQE2 assessments, as in legal practice, a case is rarely clear cut or a sure-fire winner. Part of the skill of the advocate is to anticipate and defuse any arguments which their opponent might advance. Often these will be apparent from the statements of case or the evidence in support of an interim application. So, in relation to an application to set aside judgment in default, the claimant might point to the defendant's seven-day delay in making the application as a reason why it should not be granted. Rather than ignore that allegation, the defendant's advocate will want to deploy the available evidence to demonstrate to the district judge why the seven-day period was reasonable in the circumstances and might make a submission along these lines:

> *Sir, the claimant argues that the application to set aside the judgment in default was not made promptly and that, in those circumstances, the court should not exercise its discretion to set aside the judgment. However, as is clear from the defendant's witness statement, the default judgment did not reach her until (day 2) which was a Saturday. The defendant contacted her solicitor on the Monday (day 4) but due to her work commitments was unable to meet with her until Wednesday (day 6). The defendant's application was made the following day (day 7). The application was therefore made within 4 working days of the defendant receiving the judgment in default. In the circumstances, the application to set aside judgment in default was made promptly.*

In the plea in mitigation in the criminal case study (**Chapter 8**) you will see how the defence advocate addresses the weaknesses in their client's case in their submissions, by acknowledging these and placing them in context.

6.4 Your submissions

Once you have mastered the facts and legal principles, and identified the strengths and weaknesses of your client's case, you need to transform these into a piece of advocacy. For the SQE2 assessments you are required to 'undertake effective spoken and written advocacy, including presenting a reasoned argument in a clear, logical, succinct and persuasive way'.

To achieve this, you will need to prepare submissions. A submission is the argument which the advocate puts forward to the court and it gives the facts their persuasive spin. 'The application was made five days later' is merely the statement of a fact, whereas 'the application was made five days later and was therefore made promptly' is a submission.

A common mistake which inexperienced advocates make is to present the court with a raft of facts but leave it to the judge to work out why these support the case. But that is not the judge's job. It should always be clear to the judge why you are presenting a particular fact. Each fact which you put forward should have a purpose, which should be linked to the legal grounds of the application and what you are trying to prove. A helpful way to think about this is by using the words 'and so...' to link a fact, or a collection of facts, to the legal argument.

> *Disclosure has not yet been given and there are several disputed issues upon which evidence from lay witnesses will be required and so there is a compelling reason why the case should be disposed of at trial.*

Other useful expressions to give your advocacy persuasive effect and turn your facts into submissions are 'therefore', 'in the circumstances', 'for these reasons', '... amount to reasons why ...'.

6.4.1 Structure

Having a clear structure for your piece of advocacy is key. This will make it much easier for the judge (and your client) to follow your argument. You yourself may have found that it is hard to follow the thread of a long speech, especially when there are no visual aids such as slides to keep the listener on track. (In legal practice you may prepare a skeleton argument, but this is not required for the SQE2 assessments.) You can help your listeners and keep them engaged much more easily if you adopt a clear structure and then signpost clearly. As a rule of thumb, it is helpful to set out what you are going to say; then say it; then summarise (if necessary) and tie the point into the order you are seeking.

For example, in the criminal case study in **Chapter 8**, the advocate begins their plea in mitigation by saying,

> *I shall begin by addressing the circumstances of the offence, I shall then provide you with details of Mr Davies's personal circumstances, before concluding by addressing the requirements of the community order which I hope to persuade you to impose.*

During your piece of advocacy, you can check back in with the structure and signpost that you are moving onto the next stage. For example,

> *Judge, I shall now turn to the second ground of the application ...*

The golden rule is that at any given point during your advocacy, it should be clear how the point you are making fits into your overall structure.

Remember that for the purposes of the SQE2 assessments, and in legal practice, there is likely to be more than one issue to address. This should be apparent from your instructions (in the assessments and in legal practice) but make sure that you have made a list of these and that they are incorporated into your structure. Similarly, take care to address both limbs of any test. For example, the test for summary judgment above has two limbs: 'reasonable prospects' and 'no other compelling reason', which must both be addressed.

The case studies in **Chapters 8** and **9** provide examples of well-structured submissions. The prosecution's submissions on the bail application begin by setting out the reasons why they object to the granting of bail (by reference to the legal test). In the civil case study, the claimant's advocate sets out the legal issue in the application and then works methodically through the facts to establish that the defendant has no real prospect of successfully defending the claim.

You will see that the pattern which can be followed is:

*   grounds for the application/objection
*   in relation to each ground:
    *   relevant issues and substantive law
    *   relevant facts
*   summarise (and move into next ground).

6.5 Preparing your advocacy plan

You should prepare some notes of your proposed submissions, referred to in this manual as your 'advocacy plan'. It is very difficult to speak off the cuff for 15 minutes (the period allowed in the SQE2 assessments) and you are very likely to forget an important point if you attempt this. Advocates, and other public speakers, often have a fear of going blank in the heat of the moment, or of losing their place. Having a clear advocacy plan should prevent this from happening and help you keep to time.

That said, you should certainly not prepare a script of every word which you are planning to say. Reading from a script makes your advocacy less engaging, as you are not able to maintain eye contact with the judge. In the context of the SQE2 assessments, it is very likely to lose you marks. Furthermore, an advocate must be able to adapt to the unexpected. However carefully you plan for it, a hearing might always take an unexpected turn. Indeed, even the most straightforward piece of advocacy is unlikely to proceed exactly as you had expected. The judge may intervene by suddenly asking a question on a particular issue or for the location of a particular document. They may want to deal with matters in a particular order which you had not anticipated. In legal practice, your opponent might raise a point which you have not considered. You therefore need to be light on your feet: able to respond to the point, but then to get back on track. This will be difficult to do if you have a rigid script, but easier if you have a clear advocacy plan.

To prepare your advocacy plan, you can set out the main points which you need to cover as headings, with bullet points beneath each one. You can use this as a checklist as you go through. You might include abbreviated references to the relevant documents. So, on an application to set aside default judgment, your notes might say something like:

Allegation of delay in making application

*   *Notice of DJ not received until sat (WS para 3)*
*   *Consulted sol on mon- next working day (WS para 4)*
*   *Appli to set aside made thurs (WS para 5)*

Once you have done this, you may find that you have too much material to cover in the 15 minutes available. If so, focus on the strongest and weakest parts of your client's case, which you should have identified as part of your analysis (see **6.3.7**). Make sure that the strongest points are emphasised, and the weakest parts addressed.

6.6 Ethics and professional conduct

The SQE2 Assessment Criteria require you to apply the law comprehensively to the client's situation, identifying any ethical and professional conduct issues and exercising judgment to resolve them honestly and with integrity.

Professionalism and ethics are core parts of SQE2. Questions on ethics will be pervasive throughout SQE2. As in legal practice, ethical issues will not be flagged and you will have to identify and address them as they arise. Therefore, for the purposes of legal practice and the SQE2 assessments it is vital that you are familiar with the SRA Principles and the SRA Code of Conduct for Solicitors, RELs and RFLs. You can refresh your knowledge of these by referring to The University of Law SQE1 manual *Ethics and Professional Conduct*.

Some of the ethical and conduct issues which might arise in the context of the SQE2 Advocacy assessments are set out below.

6.6.1   SRA Principles

Ethical dilemmas for advocates will often arise from the conflicting duties which they owe to the court and to act in the best interests of their clients. For example, a client might instruct a solicitor to put to the court a version of events which the solicitor knows to be untrue. It would be in the client's best interests for that to be put forward (Principle 7), but for the solicitor to do so would breach their duty to the court (Principle 1). How is this conflict resolved? The answer lies in the introduction to the SRA Principles which makes it clear that, should these come into conflict, those which safeguard the wider public interest take precedence over an individual client's interests. Principle 1 is therefore the overriding duty. The introduction goes on to provide that a solicitor should, where relevant, inform the client of the circumstances in which the solicitor's duty to the court and other professional obligations outweigh their duty to the client.

6.6.2   SRA Code of Conduct for Solicitors, RELs and RFLs

Paragraph 1 of the Code deals with maintaining trust and acting fairly. In particular, subparagraph 1.4 provides that you do not mislead or attempt to mislead your clients, the court or others, either by your own acts or omissions or allowing or being complicit in the acts or omissions of others (including your client).

Consider the situation below.

> At a hearing, a judge asks the solicitor conducting the advocacy whether their opponent had replied to a particular letter. The solicitor isn't sure but takes a chance and tells the court that no reply was received, as this answer benefits the client. On that basis, the judge grants the application. On checking the file later, the solicitor finds that the opponent did, in fact, reply to the letter. The solicitor has misled the court and is in breach of Paragraph 1.4 of the Code.

Paragraph 2 of the Code sets out the standards in relation to dispute resolution and proceedings before courts, tribunals and inquiries, as follows:

2.1 You do not misuse or tamper with evidence or attempt to do so.

2.2 You do not seek to influence the substance of evidence, including generating false evidence or persuading witnesses to change their evidence.

2.3 You do not provide or offer to provide any benefit to witnesses dependent upon the nature of their evidence or the outcome of the case.

2.4 You only make assertions or put forward statements, representations or submissions to the court or others which are properly arguable.

2.5 You do not place yourself in contempt of court, and you comply with court orders which place obligations on you.

2.6 You do not waste the court's time.

2.7 You draw the court's attention to relevant cases and statutory provisions, or procedural irregularities of which you are aware, and which are likely to have a material effect on the outcome of the proceedings.

Consider the situations below:

- A solicitor is representing a client at a hearing which breaks for lunch. The case is going well. At lunchtime, the solicitor checks their phone and spots a law report of a case which is unhelpful to the client's case and runs counter to the authorities which the solicitor had cited that morning. What should the solicitor do?

  Paragraph 2.7 of the Code requires the solicitor to tell the court about the case, even though it might appear to be in the client's interests to remain silent about it.

- A client wants to put forward evidence from a former colleague in support of their case. The colleague is reluctant to help but says that he will provide supportive evidence in exchange for a payment. The client is keen to take this opportunity. What should the solicitor do?

  The making of such a payment would be in breach of paragraph 2.3 of the Code and the solicitor cannot condone it.

- When the solicitor tells the client the above, the client refuses to accept the advice and insists upon making the payment. What should the solicitor do now?

  The solicitor must refuse to act further. Can the solicitor tell the court why? The answer is no, because the solicitor continues to owe the client a duty of confidentiality, which continues even after the solicitor's retainer has ended.

7 Advocacy: Presentation

SQE2 syllabus

This chapter will help you to achieve the SQE2 Assessment Objective of demonstrating that you are able to conduct a piece of advocacy before a judge.

Learning outcomes

By the end of this chapter you should be able to:

- understand how to behave professionally in court;
- address the court correctly;
- present a piece of advocacy fluently; and
- engage with the court appropriately and deal with any questions.

Chapter 6 dealt with the preparation of a piece of advocacy for the SQE2 Advocacy assessments. This chapter looks at the presentation of that piece of advocacy. It should be read in conjunction with **Chapter 2** on oral communication skills.

Chapter 8 contains a more detailed description of bail applications and a plea in mitigation in the context of a criminal case study. **Chapter 9** looks at interim applications in the civil courts and contains a case study for an application for summary judgment. This chapter cross refers to those case studies to illustrate good practice.

7.1 Courtroom etiquette

The SQE2 Assessment Criteria require you to engage with the court appropriately and to use appropriate language and behaviour. Some of the key points to remember, in legal practice and the SQE2 assessments, are set out below.

7.1.1 How to behave in court

In order to succeed in legal practice, you must make a good impression on the judge and others working within the precincts of the court. As an officer of the court, you must conduct yourself as such. Specific rules of behaviour apply and while a lay person could be forgiven for not knowing or following these, an advocate must do so. Here are some dos and don'ts.

When you are in court, do...

- stand up when the judge enters and leaves court
- bow when you enter the court
- be polite to all court staff
- dress smartly (in a dark suit or equivalent)

And don't...

- put your hands in your pockets
- use your mobile phone or other device in court, without permission
- speak while the hearing is in progress. You must keep quiet and advise your clients to do the same
- bring food or drink (except water) into court

7.1.2 Addressing the court

When you are speaking in court there are some further rules which you should follow.

- Maintain eye contact with the judge. This is good for your rapport with the judge and makes you appear confident in what you are saying.
- Address your submissions to the judge, rather than your opponent.
- Stay still. Advocates who are nervous have a tendency to sway from side to side.
- Stand or sit up straight.
- Do not speak with your hands in front of your face. This is another common mannerism when a speaker is nervous.
- Keep your hands and arms still (within reason). Although arm and hand gestures can sometimes be an effective means of emphasising a point, they should be used sparingly.
- Try to avoid annoying mannerisms such as clicking a pen or fiddling with glasses.
- If your hands shake when you are nervous, this will be exacerbated if you are holding a piece of paper so try to keep your notes on the table or anchor your wrists or arms on the desk.

7.1.3 Engaging with the court

A court is a formal setting and specific rules of behaviour apply. An advocate must not engage in direct dialogue with the court, as they might do with a different audience. It may sound obvious, but an advocate would never ask the judge, 'Do you see what I mean?' or, 'That's not reasonable, is it'? Make your submissions, answer any question that is put to you and move on. In criminal cases the client's liberty and livelihood may be at stake, and even in the driest civil application tensions may well be running high. While it is understandable for your client to be emotionally involved, and even angry, you must never allow yourself to become so. This is both unprofessional and unhelpful to your client.

Always be scrupulously courteous to the court and to your opponent, even if you are disappointed with the way your case has gone. Never interrupt the judge or your opponent. Do not frown or smirk at anything which the judge or your opponent says. Never lose your temper or argue back: if you disagree with the judge's decision you must seek permission to appeal.

7.1.4 Language

Formal and respectful language should always be used in court and slang should be avoided (so, for example, you should say 'ten pounds' and not 'ten quid'). On the other hand, there is no need to use pompous or archaic language: words like 'aforementioned' should be avoided. While cliched expressions such as 'I rest my case' are not used in legal practice, you will see from this chapter and from observing other advocates that there are certain stock phrases in frequent use. It is perfectly acceptable to adopt these. For example, rounding off your submissions by saying 'Unless I can assist you further, those are my submissions', will make your advocacy sound polished and professional.

When you are describing your opponent's case, you can use neutral words such as 'claims', 'asserts' or 'contends'. If you want to introduce an opposing point of view you could say, 'it is the claimant's case that...' or 'the defendant disputes that ...'.

The tone which you use will, of course, vary depending on the context. In a plea in mitigation, where you are giving details of the defendant's life and difficulties, you are likely to strike a more personal note than in an application for an extension of time in a civil case. However the language you use for your advocacy should always be measured and you should avoid the emotive ('heart-breaking') or the exaggerated ('gigantic').

Remember that the advocate must never give evidence themselves or offer their own opinion. Avoid phrases such as 'my client tells me ...' or 'I happen to know that ...'. However, it will often be necessary to put the client's views to the court, for example when making an interim application in a civil case or a plea in mitigation in a criminal case. In civil applications, the phrases 'I am instructed that' and 'my instructions are' are perfectly acceptable, but in criminal cases they are sometimes interpreted as being coded messages that the advocate does not believe what the client is saying. In that case, phrases such as 'I have discussed this with my client and he wants you to know' or 'My client wishes me to inform you' are more appropriate.

Avoid using phrases such as 'In my opinion ...' or 'I think ...'. When an advocate wishes to persuade the court to adopt their view of the case, these phrases are more appropriate:

'I submit'

'I would seek to persuade you'

'I would urge you'

The important thing to remember is that the only opinion that counts is that of the court.

7.1.5 Pacing your delivery

Many advocates fear drying up and leaving long gaps in their advocacy. Do not worry too much if this happens. What may seem to the advocate to be a long gap in presentation is often not even noticed by the court. On the other hand, if you are feeling anxious, or short of time, you may end up speaking rather quickly. Resist the temptation to do so. Going too fast will reduce the impact of your advocacy. It is difficult for the judge to take in, and be persuaded by, what you are saying if they cannot keep up with you.

When you are addressing the court, speak slowly in a clear, low tone. Practise speaking at a measured pace, until you find a speed which is comfortable for you and your audience. You can record your voice or ask other people for feedback. You are likely to find that you need to speak more slowly than you would have thought.

You may find it helpful to pause and count to three (in your head) after your first sentence. You will have heard the sound of your voice and pausing like this will give you a chance to set the pace for your submissions. Continue to leave pauses throughout your advocacy, particularly as you move from one point to another. This will reset your speed, as most people have a tendency to accelerate as they talk, particularly as they near the end.

Similarly, when you are taking the court through documents you should allow sufficient time for the judge to find the correct page, read it and digest its contents. The judge will usually indicate when they are ready for you to move on.

Finally, make sure that you speak loudly enough. If you are nervous you may end up speaking too quietly. If the judge finds it difficult to hear you, they will find your advocacy less persuasive. As above, you should practise until you have found a suitable volume: this may be louder than you would have thought.

7.2 On your feet

The previous chapter looked at how to plan and structure your submissions. These should now be fitted into an overall framework, to ensure that you comply with all the necessary formalities and courtesies. This might look something like this:

Step	To do
Opening	[Check correct mode of address]
[Introduce self and opponent]	[Check opponent's name]
Introduce piece of advocacy	Confirm that the judge has received/had a chance to read the bundle/relevant document. Offer a summary of the facts if needed
Submissions:	[Refer to advocacy plan] Relevant issues and substantive law Relevant facts
Conclusion	Link your submissions to the order sought
Questions	[Might arise at any point]
Correct closing	[Write this on your notes if you will struggle to remember the correct expression]

7.2.1 Modes of address

One of the requirements for the SQE2 Advocacy assessments is that candidates should engage the court appropriately. Your instructions will tell you the court in which you will be appearing. From this you can work out how to address the judge correctly. It is important to get this right in the SQE2 assessments and in legal practice, as otherwise you risk showing a lack of respect to the court and betraying your inexperience. The correct modes of address are set out in this table.

Court	Mode of address
High Court Judge	'My Lord' or 'My Lady' as appropriate
Circuit Judge	'Your Honour'
Recorder	'Your Honour'
District Judge of the High Court or County Court	Judge
Master (High Court)	Judge
Magistrates (lay and stipendiary)	'Your Worship' or 'Sir' or 'Madam'

The modes of address above may look different from those you have previously come across. Until recently, High Court masters have been addressed as 'Master' and district judges as 'Sir' or 'Madam'. These rules have now been simplified: on 1 December 2022 the Lord Chief Justice announced that certain judges, including masters and district judges, should be addressed in court or tribunal hearings as 'Judge'.

Although it may feel unnatural, you should use the form of address when you open your submissions and thereafter much more often than you would do in usual conversation. For example:

Judge, this is the defendant's application for an extension of time for service of the defence.

However, in the magistrates' court, you would say,

Madam, I appear on behalf of Mr Jones ...

You should continue to use these forms of address from time to time throughout your submissions, even though this will feel unnatural. For example, you might do so when you are entering a new phase of your submissions:

Judge, I turn now to the second ground of the application: the defendant must demonstrate that there is no other compelling reason why the case should be disposed of at trial.

A particular problem is whether it is appropriate to address the court in the second person singular ('You'). In the case of judges and magistrates, it is perfectly permissible provided that 'Judge', 'Sir' or 'Madam' is interposed at appropriate intervals. For example, in a plea in mitigation to a bench of lay magistrates, it would be perfectly appropriate to proceed as follows:

Madam, there are three matters relating to the defendant's involvement in these offences that I should like to draw to the attention of you and your colleagues. First, Madam, there are two specific aspects of the pre-sentence report to which I should like to refer you ...

At first, this will feel unfamiliar and might seem unnecessarily obsequious. Nevertheless, this is the level of courtesy expected and it is how you will hear other advocates addressing the court in legal practice.

7.2.2 Introducing yourself and your opponent

Next, you should introduce yourself and say who you act for:

Judge, I am Mr Khan and I appear on behalf of the defendant.

In the SQE2 assessments you will not have an opponent present, although you may need to refer to arguments which you expect your opponent to raise. In legal practice, if you are opening the case, you should always ascertain the name of your opponent, since it is a normal courtesy to introduce them to the court.

My friend Ms Baker appears on behalf of the defendant.

7.2.3 Introducing yourself and the piece of advocacy

Next, you should explain the purpose of your appearance in court by introducing the piece of advocacy. For example:

This is the defendant's application to set aside judgment in default.

If you are dealing with more than one issue you should list them.

You can refer to the parties in a criminal case as the 'prosecution' and the 'defence'. In an interim application in the civil courts, you can refer to the parties either as the 'applicant' and the 'respondent', or the 'claimant' and the 'defendant' but make sure that you use one option consistently throughout. It is usual to check at this stage that the judge has received the bundle or any other relevant document (such as the pre-sentence report in the criminal case study). In a civil case it is also courteous to offer the judge a summary of the facts, as in the civil case study, *'Judge, are you familiar with the facts or would a brief summary assist?'* Of course, you should be prepared to offer a summary should the judge request one.

7.2.4 The grounds for the application

You can then move on to your prepared submissions on each issue. In a civil case it can be helpful to set out the grounds for the application. For example, in the civil case study:

The legal issue in this case is whether the defendant has a real prospect of successfully defending the claim at trial.

You will see that in the criminal case study the defence advocate begins by setting out the order which they hope to persuade the court to make:

Clearly, Sir, this is a serious matter, and you may be minded to impose an immediate custodial sentence on Mr Davies. I hope to persuade you that a more suitable method of disposing of this case would be for you to impose a community sentence as recommended in the report.

7.2.5 Making your submissions

Having set out the grounds for the application, you can set out the relevant substantive law and the facts which support your client's position. The previous chapter considered how you could give these persuasive effect by turning them into submissions in support of your client's position. The case studies in **Chapters 8** and **9** provide good examples of these. For example, you could compare the prosecution and defence submissions on the strength of the evidence against Mr Davies.

You will also see from the case studies how the defence advocate and the respondent's advocate work their way methodically through their opponent's submissions, focusing on the areas which are in dispute.

As you proceed through your submissions you should direct the court to the relevant documents. In legal practice the parties and the court will each have an identical bundle of papers. In the SQE2 assessments you may be provided with a file of papers. Make sure that you refer to the documents provided in the course of your submissions. The case studies illustrate how this is done, for example:

Judge, you will see from the Particulars of Claim that that the garage roofs were constructed...

The sentence suggested by Mr King in his pre-sentence report is a community order...

As part of your preparation, you will have identified whether the court has a discretion or not and you should tailor your submissions accordingly. If the court has a discretion, you should remind it of that fact in your advocacy,

Judge, you have the discretion under CPR 24.2(a) and (b) to enter summary judgment for the claimant.

If a case has been provided as part of the assessment materials, you can refer to this in your submissions. Remember that when you refer to the case of *Smith v Jones*, it is Smith and Jones or Smith against Jones, but not 'v' or 'versus'.

My friend has referred to the case of Smith v Jones, in which the court refused to set aside judgment. Judge, you will see that in that case there was a delay of four months during which the defendant failed to take any steps in relation to the default judgment. By contrast, in this case, my client immediately set in motion steps to set aside the default judgment (as set out in para 5 of her witness statement).

7.2.6 Closing

Make sure that you conclude your submissions confidently. Don't let your advocacy tail off. You can finish with a stock expression, such as:

Unless I can assist you further, those are my submissions.

You will see variations of this formula used in the case study. Using such a phrase clearly signals that your piece of advocacy is at an end and indicates that you are willing to address any queries that the judge may have.

7.3 Final matters

7.3.1 Dealing with questions

As part of the SQE2 Advocacy assessment you can expect the judge to ask questions and you will be required to respond effectively. When you are preparing for the hearing, try to anticipate the questions a judge might ask and think of how you would reply to these.

In the assessments, as in legal practice, the judge might either interrupt your submissions to ask a question or wait until you have finished. Either way, you should be ready to deal with a question, which can be easier said than done. Some questions are routine; you may be asked to refer the judge to the correct part of a document or page in the bundle. The trick here is to take your time to locate this; check that the judge has found it and has an opportunity to read it, if necessary. Then continue with your submissions. If you have lost your place, your advocacy plan will help.

More challengingly, you may be asked to expand on a point which you have (deliberately or accidentally) glided over in your submissions. Answering such a question can be tricky, either because it addresses one of the weaker points of your case, or because, on the spot, you cannot think of an answer. What you must not do is to make up evidence simply to fill in the gap. If you do not have instructions on a particular point you must say so. If you cannot immediately think of an answer but come up with one as you are continuing with your submissions, you can return to the point at the end: *'Judge, to revert to your question about ...* (and then deal with the point)'.

7.3.2 Conditional orders

If your client is unlikely to get an outright win, it is sensible to take their instructions on a conditional order, which is essentially a fallback position. For example, in a bail application in a criminal case, you might invite the court to grant bail with conditions as to residency.

In a civil claim, remember that when the court makes an order it may make it subject to conditions. For example, in an application for summary judgment, the court may make a conditional order where it is possible, but not probable, that the claim or defence may succeed. The applicant will be allowed to continue with the litigation provided that they pay a sum of money into court or take a specified step in relation to their claim.

In some situations, particularly where your client's position is not strong, it makes sense to volunteer a condition to the court but remember that you will need your client's instructions to do so.

The dilemma for the advocate is whether to volunteer the condition in the course of their submissions. On the one hand, this might offer the court an alternative to denying the party what they seek, but on the other hand it can imply a lack of confidence in the case.

If the advocate is putting forward an alternative, then a form of words often used is:

> *Judge, if you are against me on that then I invite you to make a conditional order requiring my client to make a payment into court.*

7.3.3 Dealing with costs

At the end of an interim application in a civil claim costs will probably be summarily assessed. You will therefore need to be prepared to deal with costs, whether you succeed in the application or not, unless – for the purposes of the SQE2 assessments – you are expressly told that you do not need to deal with them.

Once the judge has given judgment on the application, they will invite the parties to make submissions on the costs order which should be made. The possible orders costs orders which the court might make are:

(1) That one party must pay the other party's costs (for example, the claimant will pay the defendant's costs). This is the appropriate order where there is a clear winner, and the unsuccessful party is ordered to pay the costs.

(2) Costs in the case. This order means that no party pays the costs of the interim application at this stage. Instead, the ultimate loser of the litigation will pay the costs of the interim application as well. This order may apply if the merits of the application are more equivocal, and both parties are perceived to be at fault, or if a conditional order is made.

(3) No order as to costs. Each party bears their own costs of the interim application. This may be appropriate if neither party is perceived to be at fault.

You can read more about costs orders in The University of Law SQE1 manual *Dispute Resolution*, Chapter 6.

Sometimes it will be obvious which order is appropriate. If the applicant succeeds in their application, they are likely to be awarded their costs. However, a different order, such as costs in the case, may be appropriate if the outcome is more equivocal. For example, it may be possible to argue that the application was unnecessary or made in such a way that costs were increased.

Either way, costs is an issue which you must be prepared to deal with at the end of the hearing and it is a good idea to have marshalled the arguments you could use in advance, both as to the principle of who should pay the costs and the level of those costs, if necessary.

8 Advocacy: Criminal Case Study – Bail and Mitigation

This chapter contains a short guide on how to make a simple bail application or a plea in mitigation: these are the types of application with which many criminal advocates will begin their careers.

You can read more about bail in The University of Law SQE1 manual *Criminal Practice* at Chapter 7 and about pleas in mitigation at Chapter 11.

8.1 Bail

The skills of the advocate will be required only when the application is opposed. Although bail is always ultimately a matter for the court, it will normally be granted as a matter of course unless the prosecution object. Since defendants have a right to bail prior to conviction, it is customary for the Crown Prosecutor to begin by formally setting out the prosecution's objections by reference to the prescribed criteria in Pt I of Sch 1 to the Bail Act 1976. The objections will almost invariably be based on an assertion that there are substantial grounds for believing that the defendant will either abscond and/or commit further offences while they are on bail. The risk of the defendant interfering with witnesses or otherwise obstructing the course of justice is also frequently advanced as an objection.

The task of the defence advocate is twofold. First, they should seek to put forward arguments which tend to minimise the risks adverted by the Crown Prosecutor. Thus, for example, if the prosecution claim that there is a substantial risk of the defendant absconding, this might be rebutted by arguing that:

(a) the defendant is pleading not guilty and the evidence against them is weak;

(b) the defendant's record (if they have one) reveals that they have never absconded whilst on bail in the past;

(c) even if they are convicted, the likelihood of a custodial sentence is remote.

Secondly, the advocate must neutralise any substantial risks by putting forward a sensible package of conditions, such as a surety combined with a condition of residence, which will be sufficient to persuade the bench that it can afford to take a risk and grant bail. Although s 4 of the Bail Act 1976 is supposed to secure a right to bail, in reality if a prosecutor raises substantial grounds for withholding bail, the defence advocate has a difficult task upholding that right.

In legal practice, an effective application therefore requires as much advance preparation as the circumstances permit. If you can produce an appropriate package of conditions to the CPS before the hearing, you may be able to persuade it to withdraw its objections.

In the SQE2 assessment you should consider the information contained in your instructions about both the offence and the defendant and anything that is indicated about the client's personal circumstances and the existence of any potential sureties.

So far as the actual application itself is concerned, there are three things to bear in mind:

(a) Structure the application in such a way that each prosecution objection is countered in a logical sequence, and conclude with any package of conditions you wish to put forward.

(b) Keep the application as short as circumstances permit and remember that courts usually have a long list of cases to hear.

(c) Tailor the application to the individual client. Magistrates are often offered the same platitudes whatever the nature of the application, such as, 'My client strenuously denies the charge, has a fixed address and instructs me that he has been offered work on a building site'. The statement may be true, but it is vitally important to interest the court in your client's personal circumstances. It might therefore be more appropriate to explain a little more about why your client's denial is so significant. For example:

'Sir, if I might begin by referring you to the case against Mr Smith, you will see that it is tenuous in the extreme. The evidence consists solely of hotly disputed identification evidence ...'

and so on.

8.2   Case study: bail application

Look at the prosecution and defence papers below. You should consider how the prosecution would argue that Mr Davies should be remanded in custody for seven days and what arguments the defence could advance that Mr Davies should be granted bail. Suggested submissions for both sides are set out below. Please note that these contain more detail than you would be expected to provide in the SQE2 assessment.

PROSECUTION PAPERS – GARETH DAVIES

Charge: Inflicting grievous bodily (Offences Against the Person Act 1861, s 20)

The defendant, Gareth Davies, is jointly charged with Stephen Jones. Last night he assaulted Phillip Bennett, outside the Seagull fish and chip shop in High Street, Weyford.

At about 11.15pm Bennett was outside the fish and chip shop waiting for his friends who were inside the shop. He saw Stephen Jones and Gareth Davies walking along High Street from the direction of Market Street. Both Jones and Davies used to be regulars at Cindy's nightclub in the High Street where Bennett works. Some two weeks earlier Bennett banned them because of an incident at the nightclub.

When they saw Bennett they crossed the road and started talking to him, trying to persuade him to lift the ban. At first the conversation was good natured and then things changed. Jones became more and more aggressive and despite Bennett's attempts to calm him down Jones punched Bennett hard in the face. Bennett fought back but he fell over. Whilst on the ground he was hit at least a dozen times on the face and arms. He was also punched and kicked in the chest and stomach. The punches were coming from his left and right and Bennett now saw that Gareth Davies was involved. He could not be sure which of the two men was more responsible but he is sure both were involved. The assault finished when a friend of Bennett's, John Bevan, intervened.

Bevan, who also works at Cindy's, knows both Jones and Davies. He said that he was inside the fish and chip shop, heard a commotion outside, rushed out and saw Bennett being attacked by both Jones and Davies. He managed to break it up and then Jones and Davies ran off.

The police were called and both Jones and Davies were arrested about half a mile away. On arrival at the police station both men were found to be under the influence of alcohol. They were unfit to be interviewed and left in the cells to sleep.

Jones denied the offence in interview. He said he was defending himself having been attacked by Bennett. He denied causing all of Bennett's injuries saying that Davies must have caused them.

When interviewed at 9.30am today Davies denied any involvement in the offence saying all he did was to try to pull Jones off Bennett. He said that Jones was the one that was responsible for causing all the injuries to Bennett. When told that Jones had put the blame onto him Davies said, 'I'll get him for this. He'll regret saying that. You wait until I catch up with him.'

As a result of the attack Bennett suffered a deep cut above his left eye; cuts and bruises to his face; a bleeding nose; grazes to his hands and knees; bruises to his stomach and arms; a broken nose and a broken left arm. Bennett was treated at Weyford General Hospital and released earlier today.

Jones, who has no previous convictions, was granted unconditional bail. He is due to appear before Weyford Magistrates' Court in seven days' time.

Previous convictions:

4 years ago	ABH	Fined £500;
		Compensation £70
	Absconding	Fined £100
3 years ago	Criminal damage	Community sentence with a supervision requirement
	Absconding	Fined £75
18 months ago	ABH	3 months' imprisonment

Antecedents:

Aged 27, married (separated from his wife), unemployed, previous employment all casual – barman, bouncer etc. After his marriage break-up some three months ago he has slept on friends' floors and in their spare rooms. He is staying with friends at the moment but has to move out by the end of the week. Previous offences all alcohol related.

The case will be adjourned. Apply for a remand in custody for seven days.

DEFENCE PAPERS

Mr Davies says:

I live with friends at 36 Town Lane, Weyford.

THE OFFENCE

I am charged jointly with Stephen Jones with inflicting grievous bodily harm on Philip Bennett. I wish to plead not guilty.

Last night I went out for a drink at the Ship public house in the High Street and met Stephen Jones there. I used to go out with him a lot. We used to go to Cindy's nightclub but about two weeks ago we both got banned by the bouncer there called Philip Bennett. Stephen got hammered and started hitting on some girls who didn't like it. The girls complained and Bennett became involved. There was an argument and Stephen threatened him. I wasn't involved but because I was with Stephen I got barred as well.

After having a few pints in the Ship we were walking along the High Street on the way home. We saw Bennett outside the Seagull fish and chip shop with a group of girls and Stephen said that we should try to persuade Bennett to let us back into Cindy's. I told him that it wasn't a good idea but before I knew it Stephen had crossed the road and was talking to Bennett. I thought that Bennett would tell Stephen to get lost but he seemed quite happy to talk to him. The girls then went into the fish and shop and one of the girls recognised Stephen from the night we'd been banned from Cindy's and said something like, 'Not you again, you tosser' and then Stephen lost it. He started to argue with Bennett about how out of order Bennett had been to ban him from Cindy's and then he punched Bennett in the face.

I didn't want to get involved. With my record I didn't want any trouble but I knew that things were getting out of hand. Bennett had fallen to the ground and Stephen was now kicking him. I tried to pull Stephen off Bennett but he just kept laying into him on the ground. Another man who works with Bennett, called John, then came out of the fish and chip shop and managed to get Stephen off Bennett. Stephen then ran off and I chased after him.

The police later arrested us. I was fed up with Stephen's behaviour and when they put us into the police van we had a bit of an argument. He always seems to be getting into trouble. When I arrived at the police station I was given some written rules about my rights and asked if I wanted a solicitor, but I didn't see the need, I hadn't done anything wrong.

I told them what had happened. I suppose I was a bit aggressive about Stephen during the interview. In fact I think I said that I'd sort him out but I didn't mean it. He basically put all the blame on me – I suppose he was afraid of getting a criminal record and decided that the best thing to do was to land me in it.

We were both charged but I was refused police bail. Stephen was granted police bail.

Personal background

I am aged 27. I left school when I was 16 and have done casual jobs as a bouncer, barman and general labourer. I am currently unemployed. I've lived in the Weyford area for about ten years. I married five years ago but split up from my wife about three months ago when our tenancy came to an end. After we split up I've slept on friends' floors, and in their spare rooms. I'm staying with friends now but they've told me that I have to move out by the end of the week.

My parents live in Scotland and will not put me up even if I wanted them to. The last time I got into trouble I stayed at Weyford Bail Hostel.

Four years ago my marriage hit a bad patch and I began to drink. Drink is at the root of all these offences. I pleaded guilty to them all.

The ABH some four years ago took place in a pub. I'd been drinking and watching the football when this bloke said something I didn't like about my team. I lost my temper and got into a fight with him.

The first absconding offence was a mistake – I got the dates mixed up. I was arrested under a warrant.

The criminal damage offence was when I thought my wife had left me. She went to stay at her mother's. I'd had a few pints at the pub and went round to see her but she wouldn't let me in. I lost my temper and ended up smashing a few of the windows. I didn't attend court on time because I overslept and turned up about three hours late.

I continued to drink and the last offence was also committed whilst drunk. Someone picked on me in a pub. I defended myself but overdid it. It was about that time that I decided I had to pull myself together. I went on an alcohol awareness course run by a local charity and my drinking is now under control.

Mr Davies wishes you to apply for bail on his behalf.

PROSECUTION SUBMISSIONS

Sir, the prosecution oppose bail because, if released on bail, there are substantial grounds for believing that the defendant will fail to surrender to custody, interfere with witnesses or otherwise obstruct the course of justice and commit offences whilst on bail. I shall deal with each of these grounds in turn.

The first ground of objection is failure to surrender to custody. This was a serious, unprovoked attack on Mr Bennett.

At about 11.15 last night the victim, Mr Bennett, was outside the Seagull fish and chip shop in the High Street, Guildfleet waiting for his friends who were inside the shop. He was approached by Mr Davies and his co-defendant Mr Jones. Both men are known to Mr Bennett as he banned both men from his place of work, Cindy's nightclub, some two weeks ago. Mr Jones tried to persuade Mr Bennett to lift the ban. At first the conversation was good natured but then Mr Jones became more and more aggressive. Mr Bennett tried to calm him down. Then Mr Jones punched Mr Bennett hard in the face. Mr Bennett fought back but he fell over. Whilst on the ground Mr Bennett was hit at least a dozen times on the face and arms. He was also punched and kicked in the chest and stomach. The punches were coming from his left and right and Mr Bennett could see that not only was Mr Jones involved but Mr Davies too. He couldn't be sure which of the two men were responsible but he is sure that both were involved. The assault finished when a friend of Mr Bennett's, John Bevan, intervened. Both Mr Jones and Mr Davies ran off.

The police were called and both men were arrested. On arrival at the police station both men were too drunk to be interviewed and they were left in the cells to sleep. Earlier this morning Mr Davies was interviewed and denied any involvement in the offence.

The strength of the evidence against Mr Davies is strong. Not only does Mr Bennett identify Mr Davies as being involved but Mr Bevan does too. Mr Bevan, who works with Mr Bennett at Cindy's nightclub, also knows Mr Jones and Mr Davies. He said that he heard a commotion outside the fish and chip shop, rushed out and saw Mr Bennett being attacked by both Mr Jones and Mr Davies.

If convicted the defendant is likely to receive a custodial sentence for this offence. As a result of the attack Mr Bennett suffered a deep cut above his left eye; cuts and bruises to his face; a bleeding nose; grazes to his hands and knees; bruises to his stomach and arms; a broken nose and a broken left arm. Mr Bennett was treated at Weyford General Hospital and released earlier today. What makes a custodial sentence even more likely in this case is the defendant's list of previous convictions. He has two previous convictions for offences of violence; an assault occasioning actual bodily harm some five years ago for which he was fined £500 and another assault occasioning actual bodily harm some eighteen months ago for which he received three months' imprisonment.

As can also be seen from the defendant's list of previous convictions, he already has two previous convictions for failing to surrender to custody. This was also in respect of an offence of violence which the defendant faced. When seen in the context of the current offence, this must raise substantial doubts that the defendant will surrender to custody.

Another factor which may lead the defendant to fail to surrender is his lack of community ties. He is unemployed and since the breakdown of the defendant's marriage some three months ago he has been sleeping on friends' floors and in their spare rooms. He is staying with friends at the moment but has to move out by the end of the week. The defendant therefore has no permanent address, nor any employment to keep him in the Weyford area.

The second objection to bail being granted is that the defendant may interfere with witnesses or otherwise obstruct the course of justice. Mr Davies is jointly charged with Mr Jones. In his interview Mr Jones denied all involvement in this offence. He said that he was defending himself having been attacked by Mr Bennett. He denied causing all of Mr Bennett's injuries saying that Mr Davies must have caused them. When told in his interview that Mr Jones had put the blame on him Mr Davies said, 'I'll get him for this. He'll regret saying that. You wait until I catch up with him.'

The third objection to bail being granted is that the defendant may commit offences if released on bail. Sir, this is a defendant with a history of violent offending. The defendant has been convicted of two offences of violence in the past four years. All these offences appear to be connected with alcohol. You may recall, Sir, that this offence was alcohol related too.

Sir, for the reasons that I have outlined the prosecution oppose bail being granted to the defendant and invite you to remand the defendant in custody for seven days.

DEFENCE SUBMISSIONS

Sir, I wish to apply for conditional bail on behalf of Mr Davies. Any concerns that you may have about whether Mr Davies will fail to appear, interfere with witnesses or otherwise obstruct the course of justice or commit further offences whilst on bail can be more than adequately dealt with by granting Mr Davies bail with conditions.

I shall deal first with the allegation that Mr Davies will fail to surrender to custody if released on bail. The charge Mr Davies faces is a serious one; this makes it all the more likely that Mr Davies will attend the next court hearing. When interviewed by the police Mr Davies denied any involvement in the offence saying all he did was try to pull Mr Jones off Mr Bennett. Mr Davies intends to plead not guilty to this offence. He is anxious to clear his name and does not wish to worsen the situation by failing to surrender.

The prosecution evidence is not strong. Mr Bennett claims that both Mr Jones and Mr Davies were involved in this offence. The prosecution allege that Mr Bennett was punched by Mr Jones and then Mr Bennett fought back but he fell over. He was then hit, punched and kicked to the body. Presumably Mr Bennett was protecting his head, as anyone would do, whilst defenceless on the ground. It is unlikely that Mr Bennett would be able to say for certain that he saw Mr Davies hit, punch or kick him. The evidence of Mr Bevan should also be treated with caution. He works with Mr Bennett and is a friend of his. It is only natural that his evidence may be favourable to Mr Bennett. It is noticeable that the prosecution failed to mention any independent evidence to support their version of events.

The prosecution argue that, should Mr Davies be convicted, he will receive a custodial sentence because of the seriousness of this offence and his record of previous convictions. Sir, a custodial sentence is not inevitable in this case. The prosecution allege that his offending is alcohol related. If that is the case, then the court may consider a community sentence to help him address any alcohol problem that he may have. Mr Davies does have two previous convictions for similar offences. The first was some four years ago and did not result in a custodial sentence and the last was some eighteen months ago. Following his custodial sentence Mr Davies decided to pull himself together and has kept out of trouble.

The prosecution seek to place reliance upon the defendant's previous convictions for failing to surrender to bail. This must be placed in context. Mr Davies did not actively abscond. His first failure to surrender was a mistake on his part. He thought that he was due to appear in court at a later date. His second failure to surrender was due to his oversleeping. He attended court about three hours late. Sir, you will see that both offences resulted in the imposition of fines which indicate that these were not the most serious examples of failing to surrender to custody. I would urge you to give little weight to the prosecution's arguments on this point.

The prosecution also suggest that Mr Davies' lack of community ties mean that he is likely to abscond. Mr Davies has lived in the Weyford area for about ten years. He is currently unemployed but has been employed locally as a bouncer, barman and general labourer. Until some three weeks ago he was living in rented accommodation with his wife. Unfortunately they have now split up and he has been sleeping on friends' floors and in their spare rooms. I have liaised with the Probation Service this morning and should Mr Davies be granted bail there is a place available for him at the Weyford Bail Hostel.

The second ground raised by the prosecution is that Mr Davies will interfere with witnesses or otherwise obstruct the course of justice by interfering with his co-defendant, Mr Jones. When Mr Davies was told what Mr Jones had to say, Mr Davies was upset. Mr Jones is someone whom Mr Davies regards as a friend and Mr Davies cannot understand why Mr Jones is implicating him in this offence. Mr Davies was also upset by the police keeping him in the cells overnight when he believed he was fit to be interviewed. He was tired and emotional when he made those comments about Mr Jones. He did not mean them and has no intention of seeking to influence Mr Jones's evidence.

The third ground of objection raised by the prosecution is that Mr Davies will commit further offences if released on bail. I would submit that this is not the case. Mr Davies intends to plead not guilty to this offence. In addition, Mr Davies does not have a lengthy list of previous convictions. He has five convictions spread over a four-year period and these do not constitute substantial grounds for believing that Mr Davies will offend again.

Sir, for the reasons that I have set out I would ask you to grant conditional bail to Mr Davies.

There are a number of conditions that I would invite you to consider imposing to remove any concerns you might have as to Mr Davies' willingness to attend court on the next occasion. You might wish to consider imposing a condition that Mr Davies reside at the Weyford Bail Hostel and report to Weyford Police Station on a regular basis. I would submit that the imposition of such conditions would remove any substantial grounds for believing that Mr Davies would fail to attend court on the next occasion.

For the reasons that I have outlined, I do not consider that the prosecution have established substantial grounds for believing that Mr Davies would obstruct the course of justice. However, if you should have any concerns with regard to this, I would submit that any such concerns may be addressed by imposing a condition that Mr Davies does not contact or associate with Mr Jones.

Finally I submit that the prosecution have failed to establish substantial grounds for believing that Mr Davies will commit further offences if released on bail. Should you have any concerns Sir, then any such concerns may be addressed by imposing a curfew or a condition that Mr Davies should not enter any licensed premises or the Weyford town centre other than for the purposes of employment or to see his solicitor.

Sir, unless I can be of any further assistance, those are my submissions.

8.3   Pleas in mitigation

As with bail applications, advance preparation is essential. Courts can sentence only on the basis of information, and although the sentencing court may have a written pre-sentence report (PSR) available (this is mandatory when the court is considering a custodial sentence or certain types of community penalty), there will often be a great deal of further relevant background information which the defence advocate may put before the court.

The Criminal Justice Act 2003 places the seriousness of the offence at the forefront of the matters to which the court must have regard when passing sentence. Nevertheless, the court is not precluded from considering the circumstances of the individual offender by way of mitigation.

A useful starting point in the magistrates' court is to consult the sentencing guidelines published by the Sentencing Council, and in particular the Magistrates' Court Sentencing Guidelines. These may be provided to you as legal materials in the SQE2 assessment.

In legal practice, the following points should always be considered when preparing a plea:

(a) Thoroughly research the realistic sentencing options available, referring, where appropriate, to relevant statutory or judicial guidelines.

(b) Take as full a written statement as possible from the client, dealing with the circumstances both of the offence and of the client.

(c) Obtain an up-to-date copy of the client's criminal record, and deal thoroughly with the circumstances of any offences which the court may regard as being 'aggravating'.

(d) If a PSR has been ordered, try to contact the Probation Service in advance of the case to see if it will discuss its contents informally.

(e) Arrive at court in plenty of time so that you can discuss your mitigation speech with the client and obtain their approval of your proposed course.

In legal practice, and in the SQE2 assessment:

(a) When called upon to address the court, invite them to read any PSR first or check that they have had the opportunity to do so.

(b) Begin your submissions by dealing with matters which affect the seriousness of the offence. Then go on to deal with matters of offender mitigation, referring where appropriate to the PSR (if this has been provided). Never read paragraphs of the PSR aloud, because the document is confidential. Instead, invite the court to consider the appropriate paragraph. For example:

'Madam, you will recall that Mr Smith's family history is dealt with at the top of page 2 of the pre-sentence report. I would particularly draw your attention to the matters dealt with in paragraph 3 ...'

(c) Conclude by 'showing the court the way home'. In other words, if you can suggest a realistic sentencing option which the court can take, you are not only discharging your duty to the client, but you are also assisting the court. Sentencing an offender is never easy, and anything which helps the court discharge this onerous duty will be gratefully received.

8.4 Case study: plea in mitigation

This case study continues the story of Gareth Davies. Consider the new information provided and what arguments the defence advocate could advance in a plea in mitigation. Suggested submissions are set out below. Please note that, again, these contain more detail than you would be expected to provide in the SQE2 assessment.

GARETH DAVIES

Following the contested bail application Davies was released on bail with conditions. The prosecution subsequently obtained CCTV footage and witness statements from Philip Bennett, John Bennett and three other witnesses who were in the Seagull fish and chip shop. The prosecution evidence showed that Jones and Davies were both involved in the assault. At the next court appearance the defendants decided to enter guilty pleas and the case was adjourned for the preparation of pre-sentence reports. Jones was granted unconditional bail and Davies bail with conditions.

Gareth Davies says:

I was not telling the truth when I made my earlier statement. I did assault Bennett. My initial reaction was to pull Jones off him but then I decided to give him a good hiding. I decided to get my own back for unfairly banning me from Cindy's by punching and kicking him whilst he was on the ground. I was drunk at the time. I now realise that it was a foolish thing for me to do and I am sorry for my actions. I do have an alcohol problem. My wife has been telling me for years that I have a drink problem. I took no notice of her. I have been drinking heavily since I left my wife. I want to get back together with her and I need to address my offending which is associated with my drinking. She is now staying at her mother's house.

Pre-sentence report:

BLANKSHIRE

PROBATION SERVICE   Chief Officer: John Evans

This is a Pre-Sentence Report as defined in Section 158 of the Criminal Justice Act 2003. It has been prepared in accordance with the requirements of the National Standard for Pre-Sentence Reports. This report is a confidential document and has been prepared for these proceedings only. Its value on other occasions and for other purposes will therefore be limited.

PRE-SENTENCE REPORT

COURT	Weyford Magistrates'
NAME	Gareth Davies
AGE	24
ADDRESS	Weyford Bail Hostel
	27 Carter Street
	Weyford
	Blankshire
	WE2 1HA
PETTY SESSIONS AREA	Weyford
OFFENCE(S)	GBH (s 20)
OFFICER PREPARING	Enid Barton
THIS REPORT	
TITLE:	Probation officer
REF CODE:	JW/DF/11224/M4/5/010/N/MEBP/W02
34 Bennetthorpe	Tel: (00002) 730099
Weyford WE2 6AD	Fax: (00002) 730220 (General)
	Fax: (00002 730720 (Divisional Manager)

PRE-SENTENCE REPORT ON GARETH DAVIES

INTRODUCTION

1. This report is based upon two interviews with Mr Davies; one at Weyford Bail Hostel and one at my office. I have read the prosecution papers and seen a copy of Mr Davies' previous convictions. I have also liaised with Mrs Davies, Mr Davies's solicitor and Mr Williams, the manager of the Weyford Bail Hostel.

OFFENCE ANALYSIS

2. Mr Davies inflicted grievous bodily harm on another man outside the Seagull fish and chip shop in the High Street, Weyford. Mr Davies's co-defendant punched the victim in the face. There was a fight. The victim then fell over and Mr Davies together with his co-defendant punched and kicked the victim to his head and body whilst the victim was lying on the ground. The assault finished when a friend of the victim intervened. Mr Davies was under the influence of alcohol at the time of the offence and was not fit to be interviewed by the police until the following morning.

3. Mr Davies told me that he knew the victim and disliked him. The victim worked at Cindy's nightclub in Weyford and had, some two weeks before the offence, banned Mr Davies from the nightclub. Mr Davies's co-defendant Stephen Jones was drunk and made some unwanted advances towards a group of girls in the nightclub. The girls complained to management and the victim became involved in handling the complaint. Mr Jones then had an argument with the victim in which he threatened him. Mr Jones was banned from the nightclub and since Mr Davies was with Mr Jones he was banned too even though he was not involved. Mr Davies felt that his banning from the nightclub was unwarranted.

RELEVANT INFORMATION ABOUT THE OFFENDER

4. Mr Davies has appeared in Court for sentencing purposes on three previous occasions. His offending began four years ago and consists of assaults occasioning actual bodily harm, criminal damage and absconding. The assaults and criminal damage offences were all committed whilst he was under the influence of alcohol.

5. Eighteen months ago Mr Davies was sentenced to 3 months' imprisonment. He found the experience of prison a chastening one and he told me that he was determined to keep out of trouble as a result. He believes that his offending is alcohol related. He went on an alcohol awareness course run by Addiction, a local charity, and found the course useful. From the enquiries I have made the course was not an intensive one and since alcohol abuse appears to be at the root of his offending then such a course is unlikely to prevent him committing offences in the future.

6. Mr Davies is one of five children and he originates from Scotland. He is literate and numerate but tells me that he left school with no qualifications. During his last two years at school he increasingly played truant because, he says, he was bullied. Shortly after leaving school he met a woman who is now his wife, Carolyn Davies. She originated from Weyford and Mr Davies moved to Weyford to be near her. After going out together for about five years they married. Mr Davies tells me that his marriage was a happy one but his wife felt that he had an alcohol problem which he failed to acknowledge. Some three months ago he split up from his wife believing that his wife was having an affair with another man.

7. Since leaving his wife he has been sleeping on friends' floors and in their spare rooms. During these proceedings Mr Davies has been living at the Weyford Bail Hostel. I understand from the manager of the hostel, Mr Williams, that since his time there Mr Davies has been a model resident.

8. Mr Davies still has feelings towards his wife. He was accompanied by his wife when he attended our second interview. He now believes his wife when she says that she was not having an affair. They intend to get back together and are looking for rented accommodation together in Newtown. Mrs Davies is in full-time employment as a waitress.

9. Whilst on remand Mr Davies has been making attempts to obtain work. He has attended three interviews for different types of manual work. He did have a job for a short while in a timber yard but he was sacked because he turned up for work after lunch under the influence of alcohol.

10. It is very unfortunate that Mr Davies has not been able to hold down a steady job since he seems to have great difficulty in structuring his time. He is in good health although he drinks to excess when he has the money to do so and I feel that this has caused many of his problems.

11. Mr Davies accepts that he has an alcohol problem and he is making efforts to control it. He says that he has reduced his alcohol intake and is feeling healthier for it. He realises that his lack of formal qualifications is hindering his search for employment. However, because he did not enjoy school he is reluctant to return to an educational environment. He accepts that he is unlikely to be bullied at his age. He says that he lacks the motivation to study.

12. At the time of the interview Mr Davies was in receipt of income-based job seeker's allowance.

RISK TO THE PUBLIC OF RE-OFFENDING

13. Mr Davies is a gregarious man, although his manner can easily seem aggressive. I believe that many of his problems relate to his alcohol problems. The harm inflicted on the victim was intentional. As the court mentioned when adjourning for sentence, Mr Davies was fortunate that the victim did not sustain more serious injuries as a result of the assault. Since Mr Davies has an alcohol problem and difficulties controlling his temper, which he acknowledges, there is a high risk that Mr Davies will cause further harm in the future.

14. I have no concerns as regards the possibility of deliberate self-harm in the community. Mr Davies presents himself as a fairly confident individual and I suspect that he will cope easily if his offending were to result in a custodial sentence.

CONCLUSION

15. Mr Davies seems genuine when he says that he is determined to address the causes of his offending. I feel that he could benefit from a community sentence with the two following requirements:

    • Supervision requirement

    • An alcohol treatment requirement (Addressing Substance Related Offending – ASRO)

    I have discussed these requirements with Mr Davies and he has agreed to co-operate with the Probation Service. He has been assessed as suitable.

A supervision requirement would focus on increasing his employability and encourage him to improve his educational qualifications or secure training. The alcohol treatment requirement would address his alcohol problem.

16. If the court is of the view that a custodial sentence must be imposed, I am required to identify and comment upon any adverse effects of custody. Since Mr Davies has experience of a custodial setting, is currently looking for accommodation and is jobless, I can identify no major concerns.

Since Mr Davies would benefit from requirements designed to address the causes of his offending the court may consider that a suspended sentence is more appropriate. Such a disposal would also enable Mr Davies to find work, thereby placing him in the position to pay compensation to the victim. Mr Davies has no savings and therefore any compensation ordered by the court would have to be paid by instalments.

Signed: *Jason King*   **Dated:** _ _ 20__

            Probation Officer

PLEA IN MITIGATION

Sir, I understand from your legal advisor that you have had the opportunity to read the pre-sentence report prepared by the Probation Service.

Clearly, Sir, this is a serious matter, and you may be minded to impose an immediate custodial sentence on Mr Davies. I hope to persuade you that a more suitable method of disposing of this case would be for you to impose a community sentence as recommended in the report.

I shall begin by addressing the circumstances of the offence, I shall then provide you with details of Mr Davies's personal circumstances, before concluding by addressing the requirements of the community order which I hope to persuade you to impose.

Sir, Mr Davies pleaded guilty to this offence and accepts the version of events outlined to you by the prosecution. He expresses remorse for his actions.

Once Mr Davies saw Mr Jones fighting with Mr Bennett he foolishly became involved. His motivation for becoming involved was Mr Bennett banning him from Cindy's nightclub. The banning arose as a result of Mr Jones becoming drunk at the nightclub and Mr Jones making some unwelcome advances to a group of girls. The girls complained to the management and Mr Bennett became involved. Mr Jones began an argument with Mr Bennett and threatened him. Mr Davies played no part in the incident but since he was with Mr Jones he was banned as well. Mr Davies felt aggrieved by the way he had been treated by Mr Bennett. He felt angry and upset. When he saw Mr Jones fighting with Mr Bennett he decided to get his own back and whilst Mr Bennett was on the ground he punched and kicked him several times to the face and body. No weapon was used by Mr Davies. Whilst the banning from the nightclub should not condone Mr Davies's later actions, it does help to explain why Mr Davies acted in the way he did. There was another factor which influenced his behaviour that night: his excessive consumption of alcohol, a factor which I shall return to later.

Sir, Mr Davies is 27 years of age. He has lived in the Weyford area for some ten years. He is currently unemployed though he has been employed for much of that ten year period as a bouncer, barman and general labourer. Whilst on bail for this offence Mr Davies did manage to get a job for a short while in a timber yard. He lost his job because he has been drinking at lunchtime. Mr Davies realises that it was a foolish thing for him to have done. He tells me that he went to a local public house because he was depressed and wanted to drown his sorrows. He is still looking for employment but realises that in the present economic climate jobs are hard to come by and he regrets throwing away what could have become a permanent job at the timber yard.

Sir, Mr Davies does have previous convictions for offences of violence and criminal damage.

His offending began some four years ago when his marriage was in difficulties and he started to drink to excess. He was convicted of an assault occasioning actual bodily harm following an argument in a public house. Mr Davies had been watching some football. A supporter from another team said something derogatory about the team that Mr Davies supported. Mr Davies lost his temper and there was a fight.

The criminal damage occurred at a time when he thought that his wife had left him and his wife went to stay at her mother's house. Following a few pints to drink Mr Davies went round to see his wife. She would not let him into the house because he had been drinking. Mr Davies lost his temper and an angry and drunk Mr Davies picked up some stones, threw them at the windows breaking them.

Mr Davies's last conviction was some eighteen months ago. He was out drinking in a public house. He says that someone attacked him and in defending himself he used excessive force. The court considered the offence serious enough to merit a custodial sentence. Mr Davies coped with prison life but realised that he had an alcohol problem.

On release from prison he decided to address what he considered to be the cause of his offending: his drinking. To his credit Mr Davies sought help and he went on an alcohol awareness course run by the local charity Addiction. He reduced his alcohol consumption and things were progressing well. Then he mistakenly thought that his wife was having an affair with another man. He left his wife some three months ago and started to drink heavily again culminating in this offence.

Mr Davies and Mrs Davies are now back together again and are looking for somewhere to live. Until they do so they intend to stay with Mrs Davies's mother.

Sir, there is a theme running throughout Mr Davies's offending. That theme is the misuse of alcohol. All his offences are alcohol related. The pre-sentence report says that unless he addresses his alcohol problem the risk of his re-offending is high.

As you will be aware one of the five purposes of sentencing is the reform and rehabilitation of offenders. The sentence suggested by Mr King in his pre-sentence report is a community order comprising a supervision requirement and an alcohol treatment requirement. Such an order would give him the help and support that he needs to overcome his alcohol problem.

I would submit that the imposition of an immediate custodial sentence, whilst achieving the goal of punishing Mr Davies, would not prevent Mr Davies from re-offending. He was sentenced to a term of imprisonment some eighteen months ago and on release thought that he could address the issue himself. He managed to keep out of trouble but Mrs Davies has informed me that throughout this period his alcohol consumption was a constant source of tension between them. Mr Davies thought that he had his drinking under control. Mrs Davies thought that he was still drinking to excess; a view that Mr Davies now belatedly accepts. You will be aware Sir that many offenders who receive prison sentences offend again because prison fails to address the root causes of their offending.

Sir, should you feel that a community sentence is inappropriate then perhaps a suspended sentence would be appropriate. In imposing such a sentence you can make a supervision order and an alcohol treatment order. This would satisfy the need to punish Mr Davies, but also the need to prevent him from offending in the future. Should Mr Davies re-offend or fail to comply with the terms of the suspended sentence then he knows that a custodial sentence is inevitable.

You will also be aware Sir that another purpose of sentencing is the making of reparation by offenders to those affected by their offences. I would submit that such a purpose could be satisfied in this case by the making of an order that Mr Davies pay compensation to Mr Bennett. Should you order compensation to be paid, or should you order that Mr Davies pay the cost of the prosecution then Mr Davies would ask for time to pay. He has no savings and is currently in receipt of income-based job seeker's allowance.

Sir, in conclusion, I would urge you to adopt the sentence recommended by Mr King in his report, namely a community sentence incorporating a supervision requirement and an alcohol treatment requirement. In addition Mr Davies is in a position to make a payment of compensation to Mr Bennett.

Unless, Sir, you have any questions, that concludes my submissions on behalf of Mr Davies.

9 Advocacy: Civil Case Study – Interim Applications

An interim application is any application made to the court before the trial of the claim. In the High Court, those interim applications requiring a hearing will be dealt with by a judge (in the central office in London) or a district judge (in the district registry). In the County Court, these will be dealt with by a district judge. All interim applications, whether in the High Court or the County Court, share a number of common features:

(a) There are no 'live' witnesses. With rare exceptions, all the evidence will be in witness statement form. Hence, the principal tasks of the advocate are to present their case and to argue for the order sought.

(b) Advocates are seated (except for some applications before a judge in the High Court).

(c) The proceedings are heard in public (unless the court otherwise directs).

The court hears many interim applications during a working day and it is therefore vitally important for the advocate to make their submissions as clearly and concisely as possible in order to help the court.

This chapter considers in a little more detail how to prepare for an interim application in legal practice and how to structure your advocacy whether you are acting for the claimant or the defendant. It concludes with a case study of an application for summary judgment in the High Court.

You can read more about interim applications in The University of Law SQE1 manual *Dispute Resolution* at Chapter 6.

9.1   Preparing for the application

Although the subject matter of an application may vary considerably from case to case, there are a number of steps which should always be taken in advance. **Chapters 6** and **7** considered how to prepare for the hearing. In legal practice you will want to take the following additional steps:

(a) Try to agree as much as possible in advance.

(b) Make sure all relevant witness statements are served before the hearing. Although the court may be prepared to accept a late witness statement, it will result in your client being penalised in costs.

(c) Make sure that you have mastered the facts of the case and that you are familiar with the contents of the statements of case and witness statements. It is not uncommon for the judge to deal only with those particular points in the case which they consider need arguing. Your grasp of the facts and documentation therefore needs to be such that you can locate them instantly. If the case is a complex one, consider handing to the judge a written chronology which you have agreed with your opponent.

(d) The judge should have a copy of the court file. However, you will need to ensure that you have copies of any relevant documents to hand to the judge, should the court file be incomplete.

(e) Make sure you have read and flagged the relevant passages in the CPR and Practice Directions.

(f) Prepare brief notes. Although you should never read out your submissions, it will help you to have a list which sets out the points that you intend to raise. Focus on the main facts to be addressed. You might use a highlighter pen on copy documents (not the originals) for this purpose. Write in the margin of a copy witness statement a brief summary of what each paragraph contains. An example of such a note in a contract case might be, 'Para 3 – Summarises the dispute as to time of delivery'.

(g) Have a very clear idea of the order you want the judge to make. If you are making the application, you should attach to the application notice a draft of the order you propose (except in the most simple applications).

(h) Work out in advance any relevant interest calculation and costs order the judge is likely to make. Also consider whether the judge should make any directions for the future conduct of the claim.

(i) Consider the prospect of an appeal should your application be unsuccessful. An application for permission to appeal may be made to the judge at the end of the hearing.

9.2   Conducting the application

The party making the application ('the applicant') will begin the hearing, whether they are the claimant or the defendant.

The applicant's case

If you are representing the applicant, the procedure is as follows.

(1) Formally introduce yourself, your opponent and the application and identify any relevant document on the court file to which you intend to refer

For example:

> *Good morning, Judge, my name is Mr Holtam and I am from ULaw LLP.*
>
> *I represent the claimant, David Mills. Miss Gibson, from Evans and Co, represents the defendant, Christopher Marlow.*
>
> *The claimant's application today is for summary judgment in a debt claim arising out of ...*

You should then check that the judge has all the documents you intend to refer to on the court file.

The judge will not have copies of the correspondence between the parties or their solicitors. You should refer to such correspondence only if it is exhibited to a witness statement.

You should then ask the judge if they are familiar with the facts of the case or whether a brief summary would assist and proceed accordingly.

(2) Concisely identify the issues (legal and factual) for the court to decide and, by reference to the documents, highlight the relevant facts

State the issues clearly before taking the judge through the documents. Argue for the order sought on the basis of the issues you have identified from the documents.

Take the judge through the documents at a sufficiently slow pace to enable them to digest their contents. It is not normally necessary to read them out verbatim; you should merely refer to paragraphs and summarise their effect. If the judge has read the papers, your summary can be quite concise. More detail is needed where the papers have not been read. Refer to any exhibits in a way which ties them in with and explains the contents of the relevant witness statement. You do not need to refer to matters that are not in dispute between the parties.

Anticipate and deal with all disputed matters revealed by your opponent's evidence.

(3) Succinctly refer to the relevant law and/or procedure

Apply the relevant law when highlighting the relevant facts. If appropriate, explain simply which provision of the CPR you are relying on and apply it to the facts of the case.

(4) Conclude submissions for the order sought

Emphasise what you consider to be your best points and explain briefly why you are entitled to the order sought. Be prepared to address the court on an alternative or 'second best' order if you think the court is not prepared to grant the order you really want.

Make it clear to the judge that you have finished your application. For example, *'Judge, unless I can help you further, that concludes my application'*.

The respondent's case

The respondent's case will be structured differently as the court should by now have been taken through most of, if not all, the evidence. Nonetheless, the respondent's case follows a similar model.

(1) So far as necessary, identify any relevant document on the court file to which you intend to refer

The applicant should have introduced you, and therefore there is no need for you to introduce yourself again. If the applicant failed to introduce you, then you should introduce yourself.

You should identify the documents that you will be relying on as a basis for your response, for example, *'Judge, in opposing this application I will be relying on the same documents as my friend but, in addition, the defence'*.

(2) By reference to the documents, concisely identify and deal with issues (legal and factual) for the court to decide, highlight relevant facts and address the applicant's submissions

You should identify what you want the court to do and why.

The applicant should have already taken the judge through the statements of case (if appropriate) and the evidence. Take the judge to the relevant paragraphs in the statements of case and the witness statements which support your arguments. Present a positive case in support of your opposition to the order sought by the applicant. Do not just reply to the points made by the applicant. While making your submissions and presenting your positive case, deal with each of the applicant's points.

(3) Succinctly counter the applicant's arguments on the relevant law and/or procedure

Reply to the legal points raised by the applicant. Distinguish, if possible, the applicant's authorities and introduce any you rely on.

(4) Conclude submissions against the order sought

Briefly emphasise why the order requested by the applicant should not be made (or at least, if it is made, why it should only be in modified form). Stress the effects of making the order on the claim and, if it be the case, that the application is an attempt to blur the real issues and/or to prevent them being properly decided by the court after hearing oral evidence.

Make it clear to the judge that you have finished your opposition. For example, *'Judge, unless I can assist you further, those are the grounds upon which I oppose the order sought.'*

The applicant's final word

The judge will normally invite the applicant to respond to matters raised by the respondent.

The applicant should deal with the points made against them, preferably in the same order in which they were put. This can be done very briefly if it is a point which has already been dealt with by the applicant earlier. If it is a new point, face it squarely and be quick to point to any evidence or document that supports your assertions. Encapsulate why the court should make the order you seek.

Closing the case

The judge then gives a reasoned judgment and writes their order in note form on the court file. This indorsement forms the basis for the order subsequently drawn up.

If appropriate, the judge will give directions for the further conduct of the action. Be prepared to ask for any directions which you feel are necessary.

The party who has won usually asks for costs, and the loser is given the opportunity to reply. Be prepared to make submissions on the appropriate costs order.

Appeals

At the end of the hearing, the judge may ask the parties if they wish to appeal the judge's decision. An application for permission to appeal may be made to the judge at the hearing.

9.3   Case study – application for summary judgment

Look at the papers below. You should consider how the claimant would argue that its application for summary judgment should be granted and what arguments the defence could advance to oppose this. Suggested submissions for both sides are set out below. Please note that these contain more detail than you would be expected to provide in the SQE2 assessments.

MARKS (TRADING AS MARKS ROOFING) v MASTER BUILDER HOMES LTD

You will find on the following pages:

(1) Chronology

(2) Claim form

(3) Part 24 application notice

(4) Claimant's witness statement in support of the application

(5) Defendant's witness statement opposing the application

(6) Claimant's witness statement in reply

Richard Marks is a roofing contractor and the owner of Marks Roofing. He has carried out work before for Master Builder Homes Limited. He entered into a contract to provide flat roofing for 50 double garages for Master Builder Homes Limited at a total cost of £75,000 plus VAT. Master Builder Homes Limited was attracted by the competitive price and Richard Marks's agreement that the roofing would be completed by November 2021.

The work was completed by the deadline and so far as the claimant was aware there were no difficulties. Richard Marks has been pressing for payment but Master Builder Homes Limited has refused to pay anything despite several reminders.

A claim form endorsed with the particulars of claim has been issued out of the Weyford District Registry of the High Court claiming the £75,000 plus VAT and interest. An acknowledgement of service has been filed indicating that Master Builder Homes Limited intends to defend the claim. An application notice pursuant to CPR Part 24 has been issued on behalf of Richard Marks. You have a copy of the supporting witness statement together with Master Builder Homes Limited's witness statement opposing the application. You also have a copy of the claimant's witness statement in reply.

You may assume that both claimant and defendant have served upon each other a statement of costs for the hearing at least 24 hours in advance. They have agreed their respective figures for costs subject to an order being made by the court.

(1) CHRONOLOGY

Marks v Master Builder Homes Limited

2021

7th March	Contract entered into for the construction of 50 garage roofs at agreed price of £1,500 per garage plus VAT.
20th April	Claimant enters site and commences work.
27th October	Work completed.
5th November	Claimant renders invoice for £90,000 (including VAT); payment due no later than 5th December.

2022

21st January	Reminder sent.
12th February	Reminder warning of legal action in event of non-payment by 19th February.
22nd February	Claimant instructs solicitors.
1st March	Solicitors write letter before claim.
5th March	Claim form issued and served by 1st class post.
9th March	Defendant's solicitors acknowledge service and give notice of intention to defend.
5th April	Claimant's solicitors issue Part 24 notice of application.

Claim Form

In the High Court of Justice, Queen's Bench Division, Weyford District Registry

Fee Account no.	
Help with Fees - Ref no. (if applicable)	H W F - ☐☐☐ - ☐☐☐

You may be able to issue your claim online which may save time and money. Go to www.moneyclaim.gov.uk to find out more.

For court use only	
Claim no.	
Issue date	

SEAL

Claimant(s) name(s) and address(es) including postcode

Richard Marks (trading as Marks Roofing) 17 Easthope Road, Westleigh, Blankshire BN1 2DP

Defendant(s) name and address(es) including postcode

Master Builder Homes Limited, Crown House, Jubilee Square, Easterham, Blankshire BE2 1RE

Brief details of claim

The claim is for £75,000 plus VAT (£90,000) for work done and materials supplied by the Claimant to the Defendant between 20 April 2021 and 27 October 2021.

Value

The claim is for a specified sum of £90,000 plus interest of £2,096.

Defendant's name and address for service including postcode

Master Builder Homes Ltd
Crown House
Jubilee Square
Easterham
Blankshire
BE2 1RE

	£
Amount claimed	92,096.00
Court fee	4,602.70
Legal representative's costs	100.00
Total amount	£96,798.70

For further details of the courts www.gov.uk/find-court-tribunal.
When corresponding with the Court, please address forms or letters to the Manager and always quote the claim number.

N1 Claim form (CPR Part 7) (06.22)　　　© Crown Copyright 2022

Claim no.	

You must indicate your preferred County Court Hearing Centre for hearings here
(see notes for guidance)

Do you believe you, or a witness who will give evidence on your behalf, are vulnerable in any way which the court needs to consider?

☐ Yes. Please explain in what way you or the witness are vulnerable and what steps, support or adjustments you wish the court and the judge to consider.

☑ No

Does, or will, your claim include any issues under the Human Rights Act 1998?

☐ Yes

☐ No

Claim no.	

Particulars of Claim

☐ attached

☐ to follow

The Claimant's claim is for £75,000 plus VAT at 20% being the sum due from the Defendant to the Claimant for work done and materials supplied by the Claimant to the Defendant at their request in connection with the construction of 50 garage roofs at the Defendant's Bishopwood Housing Development between 20 April 2021 and 27 October 2021 at the agreed price per roof of £1,500 plus VAT.

Particulars

5 December 2021

To account rendered 75,000
VAT at 20%   15,000
                   £90,000

1. The Claimant claims the sum of £90,000.
2. Interest pursuant to the Late Payment of Commercial Debts (Interest) Act 1998. For the purposes of the Act, both parties acted in the course of a business. The statutory interest began to run from and including 6 December 2021 at 8% over the base rate of 0.5% then in force, totaling 8.5% per annum. Interest due to the date of issue is £2,096 (6 December 2021 to 15 March 2022 inclusive being 100 days) and continuing until judgment or sooner payment at the daily rate of £20.96.
3. Compensation for late payment pursuant to the Late Payments of Commercial Debts (Interest) Act 1998 in the sum of £100.

Statement of truth

I understand that proceedings for contempt of court may be brought against a person who makes, or causes to be made, a false statement in a document verified by a statement of truth without an honest belief in its truth.

Note: you are reminded that a copy of this claim form must be served on all other parties.

☑ **I believe** that the facts stated in this claim form and any attached sheets are true.

☐ **The claimant** believes that the facts stated in this claim form and any attached sheets are true. **I am authorised** by the claimant to sign this statement.

Signature

Richard Marks

☑ Claimant

☐ Litigation friend (where claimant is a child or protected party)

☐ Claimant's legal representative (as defined by CPR 2.3(1))

Date

Day	Month	Year
15	March	2022

Full name

Richard Marks

Name of claimant's legal representative's firm

ULaw LLP

If signing on behalf of firm or company give position or office held

Claimant's or claimant's legal representative's address to which documents should be sent.

Building and street

2 Bunhill Row

Second line of address

Town or city

London

County (optional)

Postcode

E C 1 Y 8 H Q

If applicable

Phone number

DX number

Your Ref.

Email

Find out how HM Courts and Tribunals Service uses personal information you give them when you fill in a form:
https://www.gov.uk/government/organisations/hm-courts-and-tribunals-service/about/personal-information-charter

N244

Application notice

For help in completing this form please read
the notes for guidance form N244Notes.

Find out how HM Courts and Tribunals Service
uses personal information you give them
when you fill in a form: https://www.gov.uk/
government/organisations/hm-courts-and-
tribunals-service/about/personal-information-
charter

Name of court		Claim no.
Weyford District Register		OM1527
Fee account no. (if applicable)		**Help with Fees – Ref. no.** (if applicable)
		H W F – ☐☐☐ – ☐☐☐
Warrant no. (if applicable)	N/A	
Claimant's name (including ref.)		
Richard Marks trading as Marks Roofing		
Defendant's name (including ref.)		
Master Builder Homes Ltd		
Date	5 April 2022	

1. What is your name or, if you are a legal representative, the name of your firm?

    ULaw LLP

2. Are you a   ☐ Claimant   ☐ Defendant   ☑ Legal Representative

    ☐ Other (please specify)

    If you are a legal representative whom do you represent?   The Claimant

3. What order are you asking the court to make and why?

    Summary judgment pursuant to CPR Part 24, rule 24.2(a)(ii) and (b) because the defendant has no real
    prospect of successfully defending the claim and there is no other compelling reason why the case should
    be disposed of at trial.

4. Have you attached a draft of the order you are applying for?   ☑ Yes   ☐ No

5. How do you want to have this application dealt with?   ☑ at a hearing   ☐ without a hearing

    ☐ at a remote hearing

6. How long do you think the hearing will last?   ☐ Hours   20 Minutes

    Is this time estimate agreed by all parties?   ☑ Yes   ☐ No

7. Give details of any fixed trial date or period   N/A

8. What level of Judge does your hearing need?   Judge

9. Who should be served with this application?   The Defendant

9a. Please give the service address, (other than details
    of the claimant or defendant) of any party named in
    question 9.

N244 Application notice (06.22)   1   © Crown copyright 2022

10. What information will you be relying on, in support of your application?

☑ the attached witness statement

☑ the statement of case

☐ the evidence set out in the box below

If necessary, please continue on a separate sheet.

2

107

11. Do you believe you, or a witness who will give evidence on your behalf, are vulnerable in any way which the court needs to consider?

☐ Yes. Please explain in what way you or the witness are vulnerable and what steps, support or adjustments you wish the court and the judge to consider.

[ ]

☑ No

3

Statement of Truth

I understand that proceedings for contempt of court may be brought against a person who makes, or causes to be made, a false statement in a document verified by a statement of truth without an honest belief in its truth.

- [✓] **I believe** that the facts stated in section 10 (and any continuation sheets) are true.

- [ ] **The applicant believes** that the facts stated in section 10 (and any continuation sheets) are true. **I am authorised** by the applicant to sign this statement.

Signature

Richard Marks

- [✓] Applicant
- [ ] Litigation friend (where applicant is a child or a Protected Party)
- [ ] Applicant's legal representative (as defined by CPR 2.3(1))

Date

Day	Month	Year
5	April	2022

Full name

Richard Marks

Name of applicant's legal representative's firm

ULaw LLP

If signing on behalf of firm or company give position or office held

4

Applicant's address to which documents should be sent.

Building and street
2 Bunhill Row

Second line of address

Town or city
London

County (optional)

Postcode
E | C | 1 | Y | 8 | H | Q

If applicable

Phone number

Fax phone number

DX number

Your Ref.

Email

5

(4) CLAIMANT'S WITNESS STATEMENT

Claimant

1st

R Marks

5 April 2022

Claim N° OM1527

IN THE HIGH COURT OF JUSTICE

QUEEN'S BENCH DIVISION

WEYFORD DISTRICT REGISTRY

BETWEEN

RICHARD MARKS

(TRADING AS MARKS ROOFING)

Claimant

and

MASTER BUILDER HOMES LIMITED

Defendant

CLAIMANT'S WITNESS STATEMENT IN SUPPORT OF

APPLICATION UNDER CPR PART 24

I, Richard Marks, of 17 Easthope Road, Westleigh, say as follows:-

1. The statements of fact in this statement are made from my own knowledge. I am the owner of the business Marks Roofing which specialises in providing flat roofing and I am the claimant in this case. This statement has been prepared following discussions with my solicitor by telephone. The statements of fact in this statement are made from my own knowledge.

2. On 7 March 2021 the defendant engaged me to provide and construct the roofs on 50 double garages for houses forming phase 1 of the defendant's development at an estate at Bishopswood, Westerfield. I gave them a written quotation which Paul Walters, their managing director, verbally agreed. I didn't keep a copy.

3. I agreed to build the garage roofs for £1,500 plus VAT per garage. I built all of the garages between 20 April 2021 and 27 October 2021. However, despite numerous written and telephone requests the defendant has failed to pay for this work. The amount I am owed is set out in the particulars of claim in this action.

4. I believe that the defendant has no real prospect of successfully defending my claim and there is no other compelling reason why this case should be disposed of at a trial.

I believe that the facts stated in this witness statement are true. I understand that proceedings for contempt of court may be brought against anyone who makes, or causes to be made, a false statement in a document verified by a statement of truth without an honest belief in its truth.

Signed: Richard Marks

Dated: 5 April 2022

(5) DEFENDANT'S WITNESS STATEMENT

Defendant

1st

P Walters

12 April 2022

Claim N° OM1527

IN THE HIGH COURT OF JUSTICE

QUEEN'S BENCH DIVISION

WEYFORD DISTRICT REGISTRY

BETWEEN

RICHARD MARKS

(TRADING AS MARKS ROOFING)

Claimant

and

MASTER BUILDER HOMES LIMITED

Defendant

DEFENDANT'S WITNESS STATEMENT OPPOSING

CLAIMANT'S APPLICATION UNDER CPR PART 24

I, Paul Walters, Managing Director of Master Builder Homes Limited, whose registered office is at Crown House, Jubilee Square, Easterham, say as follows:-

1. I am an employee and director of the defendant in this case and I am authorised by the defendant to make this witness statement on its behalf. The statements of fact in this statement are made from my own knowledge. This statement has been prepared following discussions with my solicitor by telephone.

2. I have read a copy of the witness statement of Richard Marks made on 5 April 2022 on behalf of the claimant and for the reasons set out below I deny that the defendant is indebted to the claimant as alleged or at all.

3. The defendant builds high quality executive housing and is presently developing an estate at Bishopswood, Westerfield. I agree that the defendant engaged the claimant to provide and construct the roofs on garages for the houses forming phase 1 of this development. They contracted to build 50 double garage roofs at an agreed price of £1,500 plus VAT per garage. The contract between us was purely oral. This is not unusual with contractors such as Richard Marks who we have used a lot in the past.

4. It was an implied term of the agreement between the parties that the claimant would carry out the work in a proper and workmanlike manner and with all due care and skill and that any materials supplied would be of satisfactory quality and reasonably fit for their purpose.

5. In breach of these implied terms the roofs provided and constructed by the claimant have the following defects:-

Plots 3, 4, 8	Garage roofs leak due to insufficient bitumen being applied. Damp has penetrated the timber joists, so roofs require stripping, joists replacing and roofs re-laying.
Plots 10, 33, 42, 48	Garage roofs suffer from puddling and will require stripping off and completely re-laying.
Plots 21, 22	Bitumen has been applied carelessly so as to mark and deface the rendering on the adjacent houses.
Plots 9, 14, 23, 28	Timber joists have twisted and warped so as to split the felting and leave gaps between the roof and supporting walls, so roofs require stripping, joists replacing and roofs re-laying.

I would estimate that the total cost of putting these defects right is in the region of £30,000 inclusive of VAT.

6.   Quite apart from the cost of repairs referred to in paragraph 5 herein, the defendant has suffered damage as it has been unable to offer these plots for sale and has been deprived of the profit therefrom. All the houses in phase 1 of the development are to be sold at £350,000 each. The budgeted net profit on each plot is £40,000. Furthermore, the poor condition of so many garages has given the whole development a bad reputation.

7.   The claimant has been well aware that these defects have existed since 11 February 2022 when I telephoned him in response to his letter of 10 February in which he threatened legal action. I informed him that he would get nothing until the defects were put right to which he replied that he did not know what I was talking about.

8.   For the reasons set out above, I deny that the defendant is indebted to the claimant as alleged or at all. Accordingly I would ask that the claimant's application be dismissed.

I believe that the facts stated in this witness statement are true. I understand that proceedings for contempt of court may be brought against anyone who makes, or causes to be made, a false statement in a document verified by a statement of truth without an honest belief in its truth.

Signed: Paul Walters

Dated: 12 April 2022

(6) CLAIMANT'S SECOND WITNESS STATEMENT

Claimant

2nd

Richard Marks RM1

29 April 2022

IN THE HIGH COURT OF JUSTICE   Claim N° OM1527

QUEEN'S BENCH DIVISION

WEYFORD DISTRICT REGISTRY

BETWEEN

RICHARD MARKS

(TRADING AS MARKS ROOFING)

Claimant

and

MASTER BUILDER HOMES LIMITED

Defendant

CLAIMANT'S WITNESS STATEMENT IN REPLY

I, Richard Marks, of 17, Easthope Road, Westleigh, say as follows:-

1. The statements of fact in this witness statement are made from my own knowledge. This statement has been prepared following discussions with my solicitor by telephone.

2. I have read a copy of the witness statement of Paul Walters made on 12 April 2022 on behalf of the defendant.

3. I dispute Paragraphs 5 and 6 since until 15 March 2022 I was wholly unaware that the defendant was dissatisfied with any of the completed garages. I have never been given an opportunity to inspect the alleged defects and am therefore unable to comment either upon their existence or the alleged cost of effecting repairs.

4. I deny the contents of Paragraph 7. I have never spoken to Paul Walters on the telephone. I refer to a copy of a letter dated 14 March 2022 marked 'RM1' which is the first intimation I have ever received about this particular problem.

5. I accordingly ask that this Honourable Court awards me summary judgment.

I believe that the facts stated in this witness statement are true. I understand that proceedings for contempt of court may be brought against anyone who makes, or causes to be made, a false statement in a document verified by a statement of truth without an honest belief in its truth.

Signed: Richard Marks

Dated: 29 April 2022

IN THE HIGH COURT OF JUSTICE

QUEEN'S BENCH DIVISION

WEYFORD DISTRICT REGISTRY

BETWEEN

Claim N° OM 1527

RICHARD MARKS

(TRADING AS MARKS ROOFING)

Claimant

and

MASTER BUILDER HOMES LIMITED

Defendant

This is the exhibit marked 'RM1' referred to in the witness statement of Richard Marks made this 29th day of April 2022.

Signed: Richard Marks

Dated: 29/4/2022

MASTER BUILDER HOMES LIMITED

Crown House

Jubilee Square

Easterham

EH6 8DL

Tel: 01409 255600

Fax: 01409 123321

Richard Marks   14 March 2022

Marks Roofing

17 Easthope Road

Westleigh

WT7 5AC

Dear Richard,

Phase 1 – Bishopswood

I have received court papers from your solicitors and frankly I am disappointed. We have always had an excellent working relationship and I am sad to see it threatened by legal action which, as we both know, benefits no one but our lawyers.

We have had big problems with the roofs on plots 3, 4, 8, 9, 10, 14, 21–23, 28, 33, 42 and 48. I cannot really see how you can push for payment until these are rectified, the plots are unsaleable until then.

You also know just how tough things are in the industry at the moment. It is no secret that sales are at an all-time low and I cannot afford any delays in getting all the plots on the market. Bishopswood is getting a reputation with local surveyors and estate agents as a problem estate and you know how damaging that can be.

Please contact me as to when you can start on the roofs. Needless to say I expect you to do this free of charge since it is your responsibility to complete the job properly.

Yours sincerely

Paul Walters

CLAIMANT'S SUBMISSIONS

Judge, my name is Mr Holtam from ULaw LLP and I represent the claimant Richard Marks, trading as Marks Roofing. Miss Gibson, of Swallows and Co, acts for Master Builder Homes Ltd.

This is the claimant's application for summary judgment in a debt action concerning a contract in which the claimant agreed to construct 50 Garage roofs at the defendant's Bishopswood Housing Development.

Judge, do you have the bundle of documents?

[The judge replies that they do have the bundle of documents.]

Judge, are you familiar with the facts of the case or would a brief summary assist?

[The judge replies that they are familiar with the facts and a brief summary is not required.]

Thank you, Judge.

The legal issue in this case is whether the defendant has a real prospect of successfully defending the claim at trial.

The purported defence is that 13 of the 50 garage roofs installed by the claimant are defective. The defendant alleges that some of the roofs leak, some suffer from puddling, some have resulted in the rendering on adjoining houses being defaced and some have warped timber joists.

Judge, you will see from the particulars of claim that the garage roofs were constructed between April and October of last year at the agreed price per roof of £1,500 plus VAT. The total amount claimed is £90,000 plus interest.

Judge, I shall now take you to the witness statement of Mr Marks.

Paragraphs 2 and 3 set out the contractual terms and in paragraph 3 you will see that despite numerous written and telephone requests for payment the amount is still outstanding.

In his witness statement Mr Walters, at paragraph 3, agrees the terms of the contract and in paragraph 5 gives evidence of the alleged defects. The alleged defects are disputed and the defects alleged in relation to plots 21 and 22 are not defects to the garage roofs at all and can be easily remedied by cleaning. Mr Walters estimates that the total cost of putting these defects right is in the region of £30,000 inclusive of VAT and yet the total cost of installing the 11 allegedly defective flat roofs was only £19,800 inclusive of VAT. Even if what the defendant says is true the figure for the repairs seems excessive. It is interesting to note that no detailed breakdown of how the figure of £30,000 is calculated is provided by Mr Walters.

In paragraph 6, Mr Walters states that he has been unable to offer these properties for sale and that he has been deprived of profit as a result. Judge, there is nothing stopping the defendant offering these properties for sale. They can be shown to potential purchasers and the defendant can assure potential purchasers that any defects will be remedied before they move into the houses. Also, as is well known, house prices have fallen since these houses were built and it is highly unlikely that these houses would now sell for £350,000. There is no independent evidence produced by Master Builder Homes of the current market value of these houses. It is unlikely that the defendant will make a £40,000 profit on these houses in the present climate. The defendant has not been deprived of the profit from the sale of these houses as a result of the alleged defects. Even if the defendant makes a profit, the profit has merely been delayed not extinguished. It is submitted that the defendant is looking to the claimant to compensate him for the depressed state of the current housing market.

In paragraph 6 Mr Walters states that the poor condition of so many garage roofs has given the estate a poor reputation. This is difficult to comprehend as the 11 houses with the alleged defects have not been offered for sale. The poor reputation of the development must therefore be due to the other houses that are being offered for sale; a matter which is outside the claimant's control.

In paragraph 7 Mr Walters refers to a telephone conversation. It is the claimant's case that no such telephone conversation took place.

Judge, you will see that Mr Marks has filed a witness statement in reply.

In paragraph 3 you will see that it was not until 15 March that Mr Marks knew Mr Walters was dissatisfied with his work. In paragraph 4 Mr Marks produces RM1: the letter he received from Mr Walters. In his letter Mr Marks refers to how tough things are in the industry at the moment. This reinforces the submission that I made earlier. The defendant is looking to blame Mr Marks for matters which can be explained by the difficult market conditions in the property industry at the moment. Judge, you will see that no reference is made to the alleged telephone conversation between Mr Walters and Mr Marks that was referred to earlier. There is no reference to it because no such conversation took place.

Judge, you have the discretion under CPR 24.2(a) and (b) to enter summary judgment for the claimant. The defendant has no real prospect of successfully defending the claim at trial and there is no other compelling reason why this claim should go to trial.

The claimant has discharged his burden of proof.

The defendant alleges that some of the garage roofs are defective. The garage roofs were completed on 27 October 2021 yet he leaves it until a letter dated 14 March 2022 to bring the defects to the attention of the claimant. Surely if there had been defects then this would have been brought to the attention of the claimant when they were first discovered.

The claimant has been denied the opportunity of inspecting the alleged defects. Again if there were such defects then you would expect the defendant to be keen to show them to the claimant. There is no independent expert evidence to support Mr Walters' contention that the garage roofs are defective.

Neither is there any supporting evidence for Mr Walters' contention that the garage roofs would cost some £30,000 to repair which is much more than the garage roofs cost to install in the first place. The claimant contends that the defendant is looking for someone to blame for the fact that this development has failed to sell. This is not the fault of the claimant but a sign of the difficult market conditions in the property industry at the moment.

Unless I can assist you further Judge, I invite you to award summary judgment for the claimant.

DEFENDANT'S SUBMISSIONS

I intend to refer to the same documents as Mr Holtam.

Mr Holtam was correct when he identified the legal issue for you to decide namely whether the defendant has a real prospect of successfully defending the claim at trial.

It is the defendant's case that there is a defence with a real prospect of success at trial. The defence is that 13 of the garage roofs have problems. These include leaking roofs, puddling, the careless application of bitumen and warping. The garage roofs will need attention at significant cost.

Judge, from the particulars of claim you will see that there was one contract for the construction of 50 garage roofs.

The only dispute that the defendant has with the evidence contained in Mr Marks' witness statement opposing the application is contained in paragraph 3. In paragraph 3 Mr Marks states that despite numerous written and telephone requests the Defendant has failed to pay for this work. Judge, there were only two written reminders and no telephone reminders for payment before ULaw LLP were instructed.

The defendant's defence is contained in Mr Walters' witness statement.

Mr Walters in paragraph 3 gives evidence of the terms of the contract which are not in dispute. There was one contract for the claimant to provide 50 garage roofs.

The contract contained the implied terms mentioned in paragraph 4 of Mr Walters' witness statement.

Paragraph 5 outlines the breaches of those implied terms.

The defendant agrees with Mr Holtam's assertion that the roofs to Plots 21 and 22 are not defective. However that does not absolve the claimant from responsibility for careless application of bitumen to those Plots.

Mr Walters' estimate of the cost of putting these defects right is in excess of the original cost of the garage roofs. The cost is more because the existing roofs have to be stripped, joists replaced and the roofs re-laid; much more work than if the roofs had been properly installed by the claimant. A detailed breakdown of how the £30,000 figure is calculated can be provided in due course.

The defendant's decision not to offer these plots for sale is a simple one. No one would buy these houses with such obvious defects. Market conditions are such that any minor defect, let alone more serious ones such as these, will discourage potential purchasers from making offers.

Paragraph 7 refers to a telephone conversation that did take place between Mr Walters and Mr Marks on 11 February 2022.

Judge, I shall now address Mr Marks' witness statement in reply.

Paragraph 3 is disputed. It is the defendant's case that Mr Marks did know of the defects as a result of the telephone conversation of 11 February.

Judge, Mr Holtam was correct when he said earlier that under CPR 24.2(a)(ii) and (b) you have the power to award summary judgment if you conclude that the defendant has no real prospect of successfully defending the claim at trial.

This contract to provide garage roofs is a contract for the supply of goods and services. The Supply of Goods and Services Act 1982 contains implied terms that the garage roofs should be of satisfactory quality and reasonably fit for purpose and that the installation should be undertaken with reasonable care and skill. The claimant has breached those implied terms under sections 4 and 13 of the Act.

The defendant has a defence with a real prospect of success at trial. There was one contract to build 50 garage roofs. Only 37 were completed properly. Eleven of the garage roofs have defects and the construction of two others resulted in the careless application of bitumen to adjoining houses. Consequently the defendant is entitled to withhold payment until the contract is successfully completed. The defendant will also be counter-claiming for the loss of profit arising from the defendant's inability to sell these houses. Such a counterclaim will exceed the amount that the claimant is pursuing in this action.

The defendant invites you not to exercise your discretion to award summary judgment in this case and to dismiss this application.

Unless I can assist you further Judge, that concludes my submissions.

CLAIMANT'S SUBMISSIONS IN REPLY

Judge, you have the power to award summary judgment for the whole or part of the claim. The Defendant has not disputed that 39 of the 50 garage roofs were successfully completed. Therefore Judge, should you decide not to award summary judgment for the whole claim I invite you to award summary judgment for part of the claim. The total cost of installing 39 garage roofs amounted to £58,500 plus VAT making a total sum of £70,200.

Unless I can assist you further Judge, those are my submissions.

Index